AWAKEN YOUR SOULPRINT

Aditya Nath is a writer and a life coach. He graduated in business studies from Delhi's prestigious Shri Ram College of Commerce. He also pursued his passion for fashion at the National Institute of Fashion Technology, Delhi. After completion of his MBA from Wake Forest University, North Carolina, USA, he joined a Fortune 100 company and achieved immense professional success. However, his quest to seek a balance between the material and spiritual worlds, made him return to India. Currently, he runs his family's business while practicing the virtues of living soulfully.

www.awakenyoursoulprint.com

AWAKEN YOUR SOULPRINT

DISCOVER YOUR OWN SPECIAL PATH TO HAPPINESS AND SUCCESS

Aditya Nath

RUPA

Published by
Rupa Publications India Pvt. Ltd 2021
7/16, Ansari Road, Daryaganj
New Delhi 110002

Sales centres:
Allahabad Bengaluru Chennai
Hyderabad Jaipur Kathmandu
Kolkata Mumbai

ISBN: 978-93-90356-83-6

First impression 2021

10 9 8 7 6 5 4 3 2 1

Printed at Thomson Press India Ltd, Faridabad

To my great great grandfather Shri Lala Rai Bahadur Baij Nath
for changing the course of my life

CONTENTS

Section 3:
Enlightenment—Balance the Inner and the Outer Worlds

INTRODUCTION

Just like a thumbprint every single human being on this planet has a unique soulprint. Every soulprint has its own realizations, aspirations and challenges on its life journey. A soulprint is a special multidimensional 'cloud' that resides inside and around you. Nature never repeats itself in anything it does, thus no two soulprints are alike. Unlike a thumbprint, which you are born with and cannot be changed in your lifetime, your soulprint can evolve as you spiritually awaken during the journey of life. *You can be awakened while you are asleep and be spiritually sleeping while you are awake.* Awakening of your spiritual self is as important as waking up daily to accomplish your life's true purpose.

Awaken Your Soulprint is a means to free yourself and it helps you in your spiritual rebirth where you discover a new universe around you that you never realized existed before. This book gives all the wisdom and power to you to transform your life. This transformation will help you discover the unique dots present inside and outside you, and will acquaint you with the science and art of its connections. You will start making intelligent everyday choices to walk on a practical, successful and completely soulful path. This path will be created by you and for you based on your special soulprint.

With the passage of time, the gap between spiritual life and everyday living has widened considerably as we find our spiritual lives booted with an older version of the spiritual software. The wisdom of our religious leaders has not evolved with the evolution in our societies, as the tenets or commandments given by them are based on their journey in historic times. However, the challenges faced by billions of soulprints are unique and need to be addressed individually.

No two flowers are the same. You can never stand in the same river water twice. Thus, you require and rightfully deserve a customized path or solution with ever changing sets of realizations as and when you awaken in your spiritual journey. The attempt to fit numerous soulprints into the 'one size fits all' dictum had created this gap of the two worlds. This book provides the tools to answer your 'Million-Realization Questions' (as there is no dollar in the spiritual realm!) that you encounter during your journey.

Awaken Your Soulprint is based on the concept of soulful living. Soulful living is a spiritually evolved way of living, based on the wisdom of the last 3,000 or more years of human spiritual evolution. The path of soulful living has always been available to us, but it was the 'road not taken'. The principles of soulful living are the eternal laws of nature and are referred by different names, such as Tao (the Chinese word literally meaning the 'way' or 'path' on which traditions of Taoism are based), Logos (the Greek word meaning divine reason, logic, and creative order), Rit (as in Riti or the cosmic flow of energy as in the Vedas*)*, eternal truth, Sanatan Dharma and the Cosmic Law. The eternal truth, by its definition, always remains the same, but its wisdom and application need to evolve and change with time. In essence, soulful living is an evolved way of life mentioned in the Vedic literature as Satyug or the age of soulful truth. During that historic period, everyone was soulful in their thoughts, acts and deeds, that is, in their way of life. *Soulful living* is an evolution of the same way of life suitable and relevant for the current times.

Soulful living provides various tools to awaken your soulprint. These tools increase your spiritual metabolism, that is, make your energies soulful to attain higher spiritual wisdom, spiritual practice, faith and devotion.

In this book, you will realize your spiritual wisdom, strengthen your faith, seek ways for your spiritual practice as well as surrender in devotion to a higher power. Spiritual wisdom will enrich you with knowledge and awareness of the nature of the spiritual realm. As a seeker, you will be able to differentiate between *sat*, or truth, and *asat*, or falsehood, in everyday life.

The second tool is spiritual practice by which you can inculcate the habit of seeking. You have to be a seeker, not a follower on this journey. For a seeker is thirsty for knowledge whereas a follower is thirsty for results.

One's spiritual metabolism, that is, the energy one puts into soul searching, is what differentiates one's spiritual journey from that of the other soulprints.

The other tool of soulful living is to have faith and not blind faith. Having faith is different from having blind or irrational faith, for one is a characteristic of a seeker and the other of a follower. Without rationality in your belief, your journey can be anything but progressive. Thus, soulful living is not devoid of faith but devoid of blind faith.

Lastly, your devotion or connection to the spiritual realm is the means to receive unlimited energy for your soulprint. Any awakening will be incomplete without the connection to the Super Soul (or God) as the higher power that has created you, has also given you the power to create your own life. The four tools of soulful living will provide you, the seeker, with the knowledge, discipline, awareness and limitless energy to metamorphosize your life to awaken your soulprint.

Spiritual discourses over thousands of years have led to diverse philosophies, religions and religious practices. Spirituality is different from religion but Spiritualism forms the essence of all the religions of the world. Some religious views on spirituality are descriptive while others are prescriptive. Perhaps the founders of descriptive science wanted to give more power to their seekers while the proponents of the prescriptive view attempted to make it easy for their followers to just follow without thinking. Nevertheless, all religions have contributed to society's evolution at different periods of history by providing relevant 'spiritual technology' at the time. Religions have had a major impact on our lives to the extent that they have not only dictated the current national boundaries, but also shaped our daily chores. Religion has demarcated places as well as time! From the 'auspicious' time to start work, to the time to eat, to the time to enjoy and to the time to repent, all have been prescribed by our religious beliefs. Religions still dictate our calendar from start of the winter solstice around Christmas to the beginning of spring season around the Holi festival. So, to think of spiritualism as an internal thought without any effect on our physical being or life patterns would be too naïve.

However, you need to seek the true essence of the spirit in your religious beliefs and to not accept them blindly as the eternal truth. You can only do this when you are equipped with the tools to know what to believe and what not to believe! The past should have a vote in your present but not a veto. In this context, you can view soulful living as an operating software, with religions as different apps, running on it, in your mind. All apps can work on the same operating software to ensure your awakening; in other words, soulful living can be practised irrespective of your religious beliefs. However, the source of the 'real' power and wisdom comes neither from the operating software (soulful living), nor from any app (religion) but from its connection to the central cloud computer (Super Soul or God). Access to the Super Soul of unlimited spiritual energy is the birthright of every soulprint. When you assert your rights and spiritually free yourself from the dogmas of religions, you realize the true limitless potential of the Super Soul in your life. This book empowers the reader to be free from religious imperialism and thus generate an inner liberation, which results in an individual's experience of 'spiritual democracy'.

The journey of awakening your soulprint is broadly divided into three phases. Each phase describes the dots that are present in your inner and outer universe just like stars in the night sky. They are called 'dots' as each dot is a complete independent dimension having a separate centre of gravity or focal point. Each dot is a system of knowledge in itself with its own characteristics, nature and flow of energy. The dots and their connections are different for each being and this makes each soulprint a rather unique combination. Knowledge and realizations of these dots, when properly connected, unleash flow of unlimited energy.

Your first phase pertains to understanding not only the nature of these dots present in you, but also the ways to connect them to make energy flow smoothly among them. In this section, you will discover the power of five levels of consciousness that make up your complete self. At the end of this phase, you will reach the first milestone of the spiritual journey called *self-realization,* where you will gain wisdom for complete inner balance.

Your second phase is about discovering and connecting to the outer dots of the spiritual world. This connected self is called the '*embodied self*'. Since there is only one truth or destination (Super Soul), it really should not matter which path (religion) you take to get there. Presently your connection to the Super Soul or higher power depends on the religion or culture you have 'subscribed' to or have 'inherited'. 'Sat' (or the eternal truth) will always remain the real essence of all religions. In this phase, you connect with *Om Tat Sat*, or the cosmic eternal truth, for limitless spiritual energy.

In your third phase, you, the seeker will discover the dots leading towards *Enlightenment.* Just like the sun in the Solar System, each soulprint needs to shine for other soulprints around itself. Together, these phases make up the three evolutionary phases of any soulprint to walk on its own unique path towards a life filled with goodness of soulful living.

Dear seekers, one humble request, start the journey with a feeling of nothingness inside you. Nothingness as a starting point in your intelligence, emotions and expectations will make this journey fruitful and enjoyable. Just like you cannot add more water to a glass full of water, in the same way starting your spiritual journey with preconceived notions of the truth will not lead you to a higher place. A seeker who taps into this source of knowledge with openness and willingness to accept different points of view will emerge as a winner.

Each soulprint connects the dots in its own distinctive way and illumines the unique path for itself. *Soulful living is a journey, not a destination.* Through your journey of self-realization, embodiment and enlightenment, you awaken to a new universe around you filled with peace, happiness and pure bliss.

SECTION 1

JOURNEY TO SELF-REALIZATION

1

DON'T SELL YOUR FERRARI TO BE A MONK!

Gurus and yogis shun the material world. They describe this world as 'Maya', the illusionary world, and claim that as the body will perish and only the soul will live, we should not indulge in material delights. A few yogis even dress the part to give impressions of their *true* asceticism. Why does giving up something like a Ferrari resonate with spiritual providence in our material world? Can spiritual growth only be achieved by negation of the material world? Is the manifested world such a *bad* place that we cannot enjoy it guilt-free, or need to seek moksha from it altogether?

Material World vs. the Spiritual World

The material world vs. the spiritual world debate seems entwined in all religious discourses. On the one hand, we are told that if we are to tread the spiritual path of an ascetic then we will surely earn a ticket to heaven. On the other hand, all religions have their own ideas of what 'the Promised Land' will be and also how will the true believer attain it. The description of this Promise Land, or Inderlok or Heaven, has all the comforts and luxuries known to man ranging from palace-like abodes and beautiful angels as caretakers. Since our understanding of the Promise Land is limited, some religious leaders propagate the theory of seven heavens in the spiritual realm with special privileges just like a privilege Amex card. According to them, a person's moral conduct in the material world determines their access to the level of privileges in heaven after their death. So, a million-realisation question is if you were to walk on the spiritual path by renouncing all the material comforts, only to be aspiring for them in the afterlife, then why not try to get them here in this lifetime? Also apart from the promise of a better after life, what is so wrong about choosing material comforts today for your near and dear ones prior to seeking fulfilment and happiness for yourself? Isn't protecting your loved ones from the uncertainties as important as any other purpose of your being?

The Spiritual Chaos

All throughout the civilized history known to man, the young have been groomed to excel in studies and gain the best education in order to become *independent*. They are taught to be competent and strong enough to be able to provide for and protect themselves in the uncertain world. Despite our attempts to train the next generation to be ready for the world and convert any adversities to their advantage we find when the storm of failure hits their smooth sails, we can see the entire house of cards crumbling down. The young find that they had confused pleasures with happiness and comforts with inner peace. This confusion creates a spiritual chaos where they cannot decide which life goal is more important and why. The youth have been dealing with failures by resorting to drug or alcohol abuse and thus fighting mental anguish and imbalances. Other common reactions to their material failures leads to health issues like depression, anxiety, bipolar disorder, eating disorders and attention deficit disorders. On the other hand, even people who are materially successful are struggling to experiencc the same 'kick' or 'high' of their earlier successes. Nothing succeeds like success and successful people have their own challenges of anxiety and fear in maintaining their superior status or wealth in society. In short, both our failures and successes become stress points causing us misery and unhappiness!

So when the young did what was taught to them, what was expected out of them, and they even excelled at it, then why are they not in a happy and peaceful state with their circumstances? Can spirituality make a difference? Whenever in doubt, seek with your eyes open and turn to the cosmos to further your learning. Learning from the cosmos is a time-tested method by seekers of all times. Nature is your spiritual classroom at all times.

The Secret Garden

Look at a seed. It may look innocuous. When you put it in the soil, it is the *will* of the seed that makes it sprout as all seeds don't sprout under the same conditions. *Thus it is the individual's will that precedes every activity.* Some religions believe that the Super Soul just *willed* this creation into existence. The actions of the creator reassure us of the importance of *will* in the cosmos. Once the seed has the *will*, it relies on its own intelligence and proceeds with its germination process. The seed has intelligence and one part of the seed automatically starts to grow inside the soil and the other towards the outside. The roots come out first and then the shoots and for every 10 cm of the root you get about 5 cm of the shoot. This is to say that the plant has a broader and firmer grip inside the soil to manage its weight on the outside. The beauty of the cosmos does not stop here. The shoots grow intelligently dealing with the outside environment by managing their contours in line with the resources they encounter. Some of them bend due to the winds but still continue to grow, shedding off the drying stems or leaves, some plants intertwine to protect themselves from falling, and so on and so forth, every plant shows intelligence in dealing with its environment. The roots simultaneously continue to grow more and longer roots going deeper into the soil. While the shoots are providing air, the roots are deriving water, energy and nutrients from the soil, thus enabling a holistic growth for the plant.

The shoot system is like the material world. You work hard and train your intellect and create this beautiful tree of material wealth. It is large with many leaves, flowers and even fruits, filled with all the comforts and provides protection from the environment. So, when a yogi comes along and asks you to denounce all this for a higher purpose you cannot help but think about the purpose of this beautiful tree in the first place. There must have been a purpose for the tree, for it to grow beautifully. *Renunciation of the material world in this way is not the way forward.* This means that we need our intellect to be active to move ahead in our journey of life. So if a soulprint chooses to buy a Ferrari, then there should not be any guilt or shame in it. All the tree did was to meritoriously stand on its own feet and grow on it an exotic colourful flower—a Ferrari. However, there is a caution to the tale, the mere act of owning a Ferrari or enhancing one's wealth, fame, beauty, intelligence, etc. does not ensure peace and happiness for any soulprint, if that is what it was seeking!

In that beautiful tree, what we cannot see from the outside is whether it has an equally spread out and thick root system. The root system is the spiritual dimension of the being. *The roots are connected to the soil in the same way as the soul is connected to the Super Soul.* In so many ways, we connect to the Super Soul that it's like growing roots that nourishes our inner self with life's essentials. Just like the roots of a plant, we have realizations for the soul.

With more and more realizations, deeper and more meaningful ones, you make your grip on yourself stronger. This in turn makes your actions more soulful and you get firmly connected with the Super Soul. Each strand of root works on its own to make the plant ground more firmly to the soil. With roots connecting with other roots, the network of roots becomes even stronger and synergistic. Similarly, the more realizations you get, the faster your soulprint grows. Hence, all you need to work towards is seeking realizations. This forms the basis of every 'strong tree' or a soulful life.

A beautiful tree has leaves, flowers and fruits. These bounties are as much for the tree itself as for the ecosystem surrounding it. Similarly, we have many relationships and outcomes in our material life, which are for our benefit and for the benefit of others. Many of these relationship cause joy and happiness in us and many cause sadness. 'Depth' of anything comes from its movement between the opposite poles. The opposites of *Good and Bad, More and Less, Love and Hate* are important towards attaining the depth of our soul-filling relationships.

All flowers do not turn into fruits. Against our wishes, there are more leaves than fruits on a tree. Likewise, each relationship and outcome in your life has its own flavour and colour and you should not have the same expectations from everyone around you. Sometimes the outcomes of your actions (or experiences) are like leaves (mutually beneficially or transaction based) and sometimes they are like flowers (unilateral benevolence of visual and fragrance), and at other times they are like fruits (complete in all respect – visual, fragrant, taste as well as transactional). Similarly each relationship is a unique experience for you, based on your interactions with different soulprints around you. And each such experience has its own importance in your life, creating a unique 'give and take' experience. When you realize that the purpose of the tree is as much to take from the ecosystem as it is to give back to the society, then you move towards a more evolved soulprint. In that state of existence, one's material wealth does not become an eyesore for others, rather it becomes a source of celebration and joy. In this realisation you strive to attain a balance between your spiritual (inner) and you material (outer) world and not negate one for the other!

The Hidden Heaven

All the outside parts of a tree, like stems, leaves are connected to its roots. Similarly, all your actions are connected to your thoughts. Sometimes you can trace your action to the original thought and sometimes you wonder why did you even do such an act. For each action there has to be a 'seed' thought. That thought can be a deep-rooted realization or it can grow only from the surface. However, the deeper-rooted thoughts are the ones that get more energy and strength from your soul than the not so deep-rooted ones. Deeper thoughts come from your deeper realizations of the truth whereas surface level thoughts come from a casual perspective like say, your sensory pleasures. Thus, your actions to be more spiritual should be based out of thoughtfulness, not frivolity.

Sometimes during a storm or a hurricane, many large trees fall, but a few remain standing. The trees that are well grounded are the ones with a robust and a larger root system and hence stay rooted. When you see unhappiness, malice, anger, fear or any such negative emotions in people, especially the successful ones, you realize that the root system in them is deficient or incomplete with respect to their version of external reality. For if they, truly, were acquainted with the deep-rooted thoughts of life, then they would know how to deal with negativity in all aspects. In this uncertain world, there is bound to be failures or challenges. A large tree, meritoriously, would have weathered all seasons and cycles in its evolution. When a successful person (large tree) is deficient in fundamental realizations (deep rooted thoughts), then the chances of it falling under its own weight of ignorance increases. In extreme cases, when you hear of soulprints committing suicide, or resorting to drug abuse, or fighting ego battles, you are only reminded of a tree falling down during a storm due to an inadequate commensurate root system. Many of the fallen trees do blame 'God' or the Super Soul for sending such hardships their way. Our faith certainly increases in the time of adversity! During adversity, we all try to reach for the roots and try to hold on to them tightly, and there is nothing wrong in that. Maybe in adverse times, the 'falling trees' too are trying their best to connect to the Super Soul and are requesting it to manifest and transcend into reality to save them from disaster. Last-minute prayers are always important but it is best to work on your root system from the time the seed is planted, that is, childhood, and prepare it equally to face all adversities—both internal and external..

Achieving the Balance

What can you do in your daily life to live a balanced spiritual and material life? What does it really mean to have a work-life balance in your everyday living? If only love can be measured by the hours in a day, how much love do you put into enriching your life and how much into just living it?

The key to having a balance between the inside and outside worlds is to be aware and live your everyday life from the perspective of soulful living. *Being* in the present moment is being in balance between the past and the future. Soulful living is about being connected to the internal and the external worlds simultaneously and with equanimity. This means being in a state where your spiritual wisdom is working along with your intelligence. It is being aware of your soul while being alert of your intellect. This means that you can *be* happy even when you fail in the outside world! And you can *be* at peace even when everything around you seems to be falling apart. You can also *be* at equanimity with your emotions even as you succeed in the material world. All this happens when your spiritual universe (root system) exists commensurate to your material universe (shoot system) and both are balanced in their interactions. *Educating the intellect without listening to the soul is no education at all.* It is like a child cheating in an exam—how far will that take him or her? A body without a soul is called a zombie and a soul without the body is called a ghost. Just be who you are, that is, a living being with a balance of the two in a state of soulful living.

One-Sided Approach

What if you choose to renounce the world (say sell your Ferrari) and decide to dwell only in a spiritual space? Well, Gautama Buddha realized the truth about this path 2,400 years ago. His life's spiritual journey began when he gave up his princely (material) life and went to the forest to live a life of a hermit. He soon realized that life cannot be sustained on the path of complete asceticism and advised the 'Golden or the Middle Path' to the people, which is a balance between living a material life and a soulful disposition. Even many yogis and pundits, who walked only on the spiritual path were successful in attaining samadhi, which is a state of meditative awakening without any active participation in the outer world. They could stay in that state for days, months and perhaps even 'yugs' (generations, however one might define it!) as when one is in Samadhi the time dimensions work differently. It is believed that one's breathing slows down and many other wonderful life changes happen, which takes one into a blissful state. However, a happy Samadhi state cannot be the sole purpose of one's life, as in that state, one is not contributing or interacting with the cosmos on the outer level. Similarly in a garden, we do not have a plant with *only* a strong root system (spiritual world excellence) without *any* shoot system (material world manifestation) as what would be the purpose of such a plant in the ecosystem? How will the roots get to breathe without the shoots, that is, how will the body of the plant live without food, water and air in such a one sided existence.

On the other hand, if you focus only on the material world, which is what the majority seems to be doing, then due to an imbalance with the spiritual world, you experience all kinds of emotional and mental challenges like stress and depression. Material living includes activities, which are commercial, social, recreational or even educational, that a soulprint carries out in the external space. Any activity, without well-rooted thoughts, causes pain and disappointment to the doer due to the imbalance it causes between the two worlds. Excelling only in the material world does not make anyone happy and peaceful in absence of the relevant spiritual context. In this state when the cosmos, in its own wisdom, shakes you by an 'untoward event', you, psychologically, get ruffled up, tilt and even fall. You will need the wisdom of soulful living to achieve the balance in your life and give lesser importance to the material world, which has been the modern day focus of many soulprints.

Wisdom of Balance

What are the paths to soulful living? A seeker might be disappointed to know that the modern education system does not have the realization about this glaring imbalance in our life. Society is concerned about converting us into robots, which are merely energy efficient and easy to manage. Even religions as practiced today have failed to answer or provide solutions to our predicament of imbalance. If religions had addressed these challenges of imbalances, then we would not have these problems in the first place. However, all religious practices are not misplaced. But how will you decide which dictum of a guru is relevant and which one is not? The power of your spiritual journey should be in your own hands rather than in the hands of the custodians of the religions. These custodians already have their hands full with their own life challenges. Thus, spiritual reconstruction is required in all religious teachings and thinking, which need to be customized for a soulprint in order to make the current practices relevant and effective in solving the seeker's unique challenges.

Currently, this issue of imbalance is 'addressed' by the expectations of renouncing the material world altogether, that is, throwing the baby out with the bathwater! The solution offered by this system is to leave, pack your bags and move up to the mountains and perhaps give up your 'Ferrari' and live the life of a hermit! This is similar to solutions that we propose when we don't understand a problem and thus boycott it altogether instead of dealing with it. As noble as boycott might seem, it doesn't assure the presence of a robust root system. A beautiful universe inside definitely manifests into a beautiful world outside, but it does not work the other way around. A larger root system can support a smaller shoot system, but if it is the other way round, the tree will be imbalanced and fall. Spiritual realm should precede material world. Moreover in the material world, the reality or the truth might not be what it looks like. Beautiful gestures on the outside do not always come from a beautiful space inside. Hence, only living a life of a hermit will not make one's life soulful.

Once, Kabir, a mystic, along with his wife and two children, was visiting his parents in his village in Benaras (Varanasi now). As soon as he entered his parent's house he asked his kids to go and touch their grandparents' feet to seek their blessings. The kids obediently followed their father's order. The grandparents were touched by the gesture. Later in the evening when Kabir had an altercation with his father over some property matter, in the heat of the moment he shouted at his parents, to the surprise of everyone in the house. The next morning when Kabir's kids demanded money to buy ice cream, he refused. Then they too raised their voices in protest, forgetting all respect for, and obedience to, their father. Respect and obedience for elders stem from a deeper sense of gratitude and percolates into all aspects of one's life. Merely a show of respect by touching the elder's feet, does not develop any roots of respect and obedience inside a person.

Connect Your Dots

You can create your own solutions to the challenge caused by your imbalance. Your special spiritual journey is yours alone. The power of spirituality is that anyone can lead the change in his or her life through their learnings, experiences and realizations. In fact, this has been the purpose of a spiritual journey from the Vedic times!

Everything and everyone has a purpose in waiting, for them to be realized. The cosmos works on the principle of interdependence of the two worlds, and both inner and outer have to coexist with one another. Your purpose is to illumine or enlighten yourself and then spread the light around. *Your purpose is not to know more but to be more.*

There are many inner dots that you need to discover and to connect in order to awaken your soulprint. Connecting these inner dots is like connecting stars to form a constellation. You need to see the bigger picture and at the same time, connect each star in its own wisdom. The way you connect the dots makes all the difference. Maybe till now just like everyone else you have been seeing the archaic constellations in your life like the Orion's Belt or the Ursa Major to guide your path. Now is the time to discover new ways to connect the stars to make them more meaningful for your journey perhaps in the shape of a Ferrari, if that is what your soulprint truly desires!

2

KNOW YOUR SELF

The journey of a thousand miles begins with a single step. However, the first step is the toughest as many a time we do not know which way to go. This ignorance causes a loss of energy and we are unable to begin our spiritual journey.

You, however, have taken your first step when you started reading this book in order to awaken your soulprint and connect to a higher energy source. This journey starts inwards when you connect the dots of the 'mini cosmos' present inside you. This connection forms your unique complete self.

Don't Judge a Book By Its Cover

You might *think* you know who you are. There is a difference between knowing yourself, that is, having knowledge about your inner dots and realizing yourself, that is, having observed and interacted with the inner dots. And to know yourself is a step towards realizing yourself. Till now, you have seen yourself through a prism. Now, the time has come to be fair in your assessment of what you are really made up of. *Without being true to yourself, you cannot find your true self.*

At some level, you identify yourself with your name, last name, face, wealth, knowledge, occupation and many other things connected to your existence. All these attributes make you special, but these attributes are not who you really are. These merely help other people to distinguish you from the crowd. Take away the people around you and all these references will not work. For instance, a tall man is called tall only when surrounded by shorter people. Would you like to judge a book on yourself by its cover? Most of your external references were not even present when you were born, so to seek your true self you will have to look inwards and delve deeper into your metaphysical self.

Your 'soul' is your true self in the spiritual sense. It is invisible and people call it by different names like Consciousness, Atma, Holy Spirit, Ruh, Jin. Some people also refer to it as goodness of the moral self. As the soul lasts over lifetimes, it is also called the eternal self. The soul in a body is like water in a coloured glass. Until you take out the water from the coloured glass, you will not know what is the real colour of the water! However, removing the soul (water) from the body (glass) will mean death. Hence, understanding one's soulprint while being alive is tricky. However, through process of deduction it is possible to logically understand and perhaps experience existence of your soulprint and use this spiritual wisdom to help realize your inner reality. In a way, seeking your soul is just like falling in love with someone. The person in love knows of its truth with all his or her heart and mind but finds it difficult to explain to others what it really is. Once you are set upon the goal of finding your soulprint, you can walk towards awakening your soulprint.

Lord Shiva, the Super Soul

The Vedic wisdom describes the soul by identifying *what it is not*. This is an important realization because it is impossible to describe something (the soul) that does not have any external references. Physical traits like length, breadth, weight, colour, temperature, texture cannot describe it. Even non-physical traits such as name, family name cannot identify it. The Vedas describe Lord Shiva as a multidimensional cloud of wisdom and spirit in human form. The literal meaning of the name of Lord Shiva is 'that which is not'. This existence is described in 'Shivoham Shivoham', a beautiful prayer for Lord Shiva, which identifies Lord Shiva as the Super Soul, and, in essence, describes the characteristics of a soul. We *are not* the Super Soul, but the characteristics of our soul come from that of the Super Soul. Our existence is like a drop of water (our soul) in the ocean (Super Soul). The translated verses of Shivoham Shivoham are hereunder:

> I am not the mind, nor the intellect, nor the ego,
> nor the money,
> I am not the ears, nor the skin,
> Nor the nose nor the eyes,
> I am not the space, not the Earth,
> Not the fire, not the water nor the wind,
> I am not the breath, nor the five elements,
> I am not the matter, nor the five sheaths of self,
> Nor am I the speech, nor the hands, nor the feet,
> There is no like nor dislike in me, No greed nor delusion,
> I know no pride no jealousy, I have no duty,
> No desire of wealth, no lust nor liberation,
> No virtue nor vice, no pleasure nor pain,
> I need no mantras, no pilgrimage, no scriptures nor rituals,
> I am not the experience, nor the experience itself,
> I have no fear of death, no caste no creed,
> I have no father, no mother for I was never born,
> I am not a relative, nor a friend,
> Nor a teacher, nor a student,

I am devoid of duality, my form is formless,
I exist everywhere pervading all senses,
I am neither attached, nor free nor captive,
I am the form of consciousness and bliss.
I am the Eternal Shiva...

The Complete Self

After you exclude the above characteristics used to identify yourself, the remainder (of your existence) can be called your soul. Your complete self consists of five dots:

- the body,
- the life breath,
- the emotion (mind),
- the intellect and
- the soul.

The body is the part that can be seen, the mind is all that you can feel and the intellect is all you think and analyse. Breath connects the four dots with each other. By the process of elimination, referred to as 'Neti- Neti' in the Vedas, meaning 'Not This, Not This', of these four dots, you can discover the remaining dot—your soul. Together, these dots make up your unique soulprint, which everyone needs to discover for themselves.

The Body

The body *dot* is the physical state of the human body. It has many subparts like the five senses, the heart, the brain and numerous systems working together like a perfect machine. While different exercise regimes like yoga and Tai Chi, focus on toning the body; different alternative medicines, like ayurveda, naturopathy and acupuncture, ensure nourishment of the body. The body is very important as it connects your inner world with the outer world, and enriches your experiences of the outer world. Hence, it is important to maintain and nourish this dot as only in a healthy body could the other four dots reside healthily.

The body dot dimension encompasses 'soft' attributes like your name, your position in society, your relationships and your goodwill. Different relationships and roles like that of a father, a mother, a sister, a brother or a friend are all in context of the body dot. Even your professional status, like that of a teacher, a doctor, a priest, or a boss, is part of your identity and is external in nature.

The 'hard' attributes of the body's identity include your physical body and your material possessions in the material world. These attributes can be amassed over a period of time but are susceptible to loss within a blink of an eye. Both these hard and soft attributes are nothing more than extensions of your physical body dot. These attributes are lost due to the body's perishable nature. When you will 'depart', that is, when your soul 'passes away' from your body, your body dot, which gets left behind, gets destroyed, and your material wealth gets instantly transferred to others. Your near and dear ones who are connected to you through your body become grief-stricken due to the physical loss of your existence.

The Mind

The mind dot or the emotive identity refers to the 'feelings' such as pain, love, envy, pride or excitement that you experience. Feelings exist and prosper in your emotive self, which is also commonly referred to as the mind. This emotive dot is enriched by your social interactions and creates desires, whims and fancies for your existence. The emotive self feels satisfied when such desires get fulfilled. After all, as Aristotle once said 'Man is by nature a social animal'. Behavioural sciences like sociology, psychology and cognitive sciences form the science of how the emotive self works.

Your emotive self is the invisible and perceptive self, which exists in you as life energy. It is a very important and powerful dot for energy generation and distribution throughout your physical self. In effect, the emotive body causes the movement of your life energy (blood flow) in all the cells of your body dot.

An integral part of the emotive dot is the heart, which pumps life to all the parts of your body, thus providing energy for the bodily functions. Its function is very mechanical in nature, but it is your emotive self that pulls its strings. When you receive any favourable news your emotive dot 'feels' excited and the body pumps more blood, and conversely when you receive any unfavourable information you 'feel' low and less blood is pumped by the heart, causing loss of energy. Thus, it is commonly believed that your emotions reside in your heart. The heart is commonly associated with many feelings and emotions like love (sweetheart) or fear (small hearted) or stress (weak heart) or compassion (big heart). This is because the heart supplies energy to the body by beating faster or slower based on the emotive dot. The emotive self might have its centre of universe in the heart, but is much bigger and wider in its existence. Your intellect can override your emotive self and take control to execute the actions of your body dot but it is only when you put your 'heart into a thing' along with the intellect, that your energy levels and execution capabilities are the highest.

The Breath

The life breath dot also referred to as the 'breath' connects all the other four dots to make a complete self. Life breath is not the same as breathing as breathing can be fast or slow or deep or shallow, whereas life breath is constant. Moreover, life breath existed in your body even before you began to breathe. When a foetus is conceived in the womb, it gets its life breath from its mother's embryo sac. However, the physical act of breathing from the nostrils starts after one's birth. The act of breathing does many important functions for you, such as providing oxygen to all your body parts.

Spiritual function of life's breath is to connect all the other four dots together in your awareness. None of the other four dots can exist in isolation of each other and that gives life breath a unique importance in your identity. In other words, it is the invisible backbone of your spiritual self.

The Intellect

The intellect dot has its centre of gravity in the brain, but it resides in every cell of the body. All the cells regenerate periodically, which cannot be possible without intelligence coded into them. Brain is like the hardware of a computer and the intellect is like its software and intelligence is its computing power. The intellect assimilates information and sends signals to your body and directs it into action. As the intellect evolves gaining more intelligence, the higher contemplations lead to deeper thinking. The Intelligence Quotient or IQ denotes the wealth of your intelligence. The intellect's job is to differentiate, deduce, induce and extrapolate information, so you can take intelligent decisions. The intellect dot interacts with the other three inner dots to rationalize and make their flows more effective. It 'listens' to your body dot, life breath dot and your emotive dot to fulfil their sensory demands with intelligent actions. The intellect dot controls the voluntary and involuntary functions of the body. It also takes most effective and efficient decisions for the self to survive and thrive in the cosmos. To take any decision, the intellect needs information from its environment and to that end, it uses the five sensory signals of sight, touch, taste, hearing and smell. Based on the information gathered by these signals, the intellect decides and directs the body and even works towards physically changing your external environment.

The intellect and the emotive dots are called the perceptive bodies and have different characteristics from the body dot. Unlike the body dot, the perceptive bodies are invisible to the naked eye. The body dot not only refers to the body weight and features, but also encompasses the material world we are living in. These physical things can be destroyed, stolen or even depleted without our wish or knowledge whereas the perceptive bodies get created or destroyed, purely based on our thoughts. The body dot is governed by the principles of the material world, which in essence makes life a zero sum game and limited in existence. This means that in material world, one person's gain leads to another person's loss, as these attributes are not expandable. However, our perceptive bodies cannot be destroyed or stolen. They work on the principles of the spiritual realm that in essence makes life a win-win situation of limitless existence. This means that in spiritual science by sharing your emotions and intelligence you can increase the existence of these perceptive bodies. Unlike the body dot, which is a finite state, perceptive bodies are infinite. Just like a candle can light many other candles without any loss of brightness to it, you too can spread the light with your positive emotions and intelligence when you share or apply them. However, the perceptive bodies are lost when you die, so it is of no use expanding them without using or sharing them with others!

The Soul

The soul dot or consciousness is also referred to as your eternal self. As the soul is indescribable and invisible, its existence and characteristics might confuse a seeker. One could confuse it with intellect or emotive dot and can live his or her life in such ignorance.

The soul dot is constantly *witnessing* all your experiences. Like a *silent observer*, the soul observes the decisions of the intellect. Your body is like a car, with your emotive self being its driver stepping on the gas pedal, your intellect is the navigator, navigating the car and your soul is the passenger on the back seat, for whom the car exists, observing everything in both inside and outside environments.

Thus, your body must listen to your emotive dot for its energy needs; the emotive dot must listen to your intellect for its rationality in using the energy most efficiently and effectively. And your intellect must follow your soul for envisioning a purpose for your complete self. This wisdom is encapsulated in the Bhagavad Gita, Chapter 3, verse 42, as follows:

> *Indriyāṇi parāṇyāhur indriyebhyaḥ para ṁanaḥ*
> *manasas tu parā buddhir yo buddheḥ paratas tu saḥ*

This means that the senses are superior to the body; the mind is superior to the senses; the intellect is superior to the mind and the soul is superior to the intellect.

It is between the intellect and the emotive dots that you spend most of your everyday life, where your emotive dot creates desires and your intellect works to satiate them. The emotive dot helps you choose what you like and want to do. The intellect differentiates, contemplates, measures and balances all the dots to decide what you should do. Your soul's role is to aspire for a higher state for your complete self to exist and to observe your journey towards it. The soul's purpose is to lay down a vision for its own evolution. *The intellect gathers intelligence through knowledge and understanding, and the soul gathers spiritual wisdom through its realizations.* Thus, each soulprint is different as all the five dots are unique and even the connections and interactions of these dots are peculiar to each individual.

A Million-Realization Question

How can you 'see' the salt in the water without tasting it? It is a 'Million-Realization Learning' to know the difference between your perceptive body (the intellect, the emotive dots) and your soul dot.

You can be aware of your soul dot at all times—when you are awake, asleep, in deep sleep and even during half sleep. You can experience that your soul is present when you dream at night and see yourself as an observer to the dream. When later you recall the dream, then whose perspective do you think you are 'watching' or narrating the events of the dream from? Like a story, the dream is played in your brain and your soul is right there sitting in the audience at that time observing the sequence of events at play. How many times have you woken up in the morning trying to *understand* what you had seen in your dream?

In your dreams, your soul is witnessing your choices in different scenarios that the intellect has conjured for it. And that is exactly the role of the soul. The role of the soul is to witness everything that your intellect conjures up, and in the process the soul increases its realizations and becomes a more evolved soul. *Realization is the currency of the soul and consciousness is its wealth.* This exists in a multidimensional and timeless space. Anyone can describe the series of events of a story, but living the experience is a different realization for the observer. Your soul and consciousness are eternal and unlike the other dots it doesn't die when your other four dots get destroyed. The soul dot along with its spiritual wisdom carries on and gets transferred to our next lifetime, leaving everything else behind in this lifetime. Just like the Super Soul, the soul dot is both indescribable and indestructible.

Milestones till Tombstone

The soul, on rebirth, enters a mother's womb anytime after a child is conceived. In this way your soul becomes part of your present lifetime even before the intellect and body are completely formed. Your soul plans its new destinations for its current lifetime based on the consciousness (realizations) from its previous lifetimes. Just like we choose our mode of transportation before embarking on a long journey, the soul '*wills*' the formation of your inner dots for this life's journey. It takes time to learn how to expertly drive a car over regular and rough terrain. Moreover, when we reach the destination (a life goal), only then we can see the new horizons that we further aspire to visit and the *final* destination always lays ahead in our spiritual journey. Similarly we spend our lifetime chasing (and fulfilling) our life goals and as one want gets satisfied we seek other. Its only when we reach the twilight of our life we start to focus on our spiritual self, in order to carry its 'wealth' to our next lifetime. This *new* realization at time of our departure ignites feelings of philanthropy and compassion for the universe. This journey is described in the Vedas as Chaturashram or the four stages or milestones of a human life.

The first stage is Brahmacharya ashram or the life of a bachelor student, which is expected to last for the first twenty-five years of one's life. It is followed by the second stage of Grihastha ashram or the life of the married householder, which lasts up to 50th year, followed by Vanaprastha ashram or the life of detachment from the family, which extends to seventy-fifth year. Finally we experience the Sanayasa ashram, where one completely renounces the world and connects with the Universe (Super Soul) in entirety. However, in soulful living you do not wait for your last leg of life to become soulful; you try to inculcate the spiritual wisdom, practice, faith and devotion in each of life's moments. In these modern times, everyone is living in one of these stages but has a lot of catching up to do to awaken their soulfulness, before they move on to their next life stage or lifetime.

The Secret Sauce of Spiritual Evolution

Just as there is spiritual wisdom for the soul, there is intelligence for the intellect, emotive quotient for the emotive dot and material wealth (including the hard and soft attributes) for the body dot. All the dots have their respective wealth, uses and purposes. The secret sauce of your spiritual evolution lies in these inter-connections and the power play within your inner dots. Like all the relationships in your life, these internal relationships of the dots too have strings of love, care, dependence, hate, power struggle, etc. and are as complex as one can imagine! Your understanding should be on two levels of these connections–one, what the relationship is currently in your life and the other, what it should be to help you awaken?

Let's look at the relationship of, say, the intellect dot with the soul. Intellect is the navigator in the material world. You begin working on enhancing your intelligence from the time you were born and used it to gather knowledge and information required to live in the world. On learning the ropes, of cause and consequence in one's life, the intellect becomes successful and takes unilateral decisions without paying attention to its originator, the soul. The intellect begins to run like a wild horse without the soul's reins to control it. Thus, you consider the intellect to be the sole boss of your existence and you measure your self by the material world yardsticks of money, fame or beauty and in essence become outwardly focused, thereby undermining your soul completely.

As per the Upanishads, when the intellect dot, the emotive dot and the physical body, all act together without connection to the soul, then ego is formed. *Ego is the supremacy of the self without the soul.* Egoistic thoughts are primarily focused on self-glorification and self-gratification whereas soulful thoughts are primarily focused towards a better ecosystem for everyone. When you give more importance to your other inner dots over your soul dot then you become egotistical and self-consuming. And when you give importance to your soul dot especially over the other dots then you experience compassion and altruism! For instance, when you donate something and have your name written on it for everyone to see or publicize your donation then you are feeding your ego by accumulating material wealth in the form of goodwill in the outer world. Whereas when you donate anonymously, then you are feeding your soul whose true purpose is to treat all fellow souls as its own. After all, you do not put names of the users on your 'house' items, as everyone is part of your family.

Unfortunately, the modern world is driven mainly by the intellect, which works on the concept of I, me and myself. Due to this, the Vedas refer to the current era as Kalyug. While Satyug is referred to as the age of soulful living, Kalyug is the age of intellectual supremacy. Satyug ceased to exist when we forgot that our soul is the master of our intellect. The intellect dot is unable to understand feelings of compassion, peace, mercy and love. It is thus unable to contemplate issues that are for the greater benefit of the ecosystem. Nature, however, always works on the principle of compassion and love. When we see the ecosystem working in perfect harmony and developing into a beautiful space, where different energies are working together for maximizing collective gain, we witness soulful living in motion. In such a state, everyone is coexisting peacefully and realizing their full potential.

Spiritual Economics

Even from a rational point of view, soulful living makes more sense. On the one hand, there was Adam Smith, the father of modern economics, who advocated only individual maximization, or self-focus to be the best way forward for creation of '*wealth of nations*'. On the other hand, we had Dr. John F. Nash's *beautiful mind*, advocating 'equilibrium at sub-optimum level' where an individual's maximization should come after the maximization of his group or the ecosystem. He stated that it is in the interest of the individual himself to work towards maximization of the ecosystem and within that framework the person will attain a higher living for himself.

We have wonderful examples of great intelligent leaders like Mother Teresa, Mahatma Gandhi and Gautama Buddha, who kept their interests secondary for the greater good of humanity and as a result lived extra ordinary lives themselves. Soulful living is about making your soul the master of your intellect and when this happens, the other dots work towards making you experience a higher path.

The soul is eternal, which by definition, means that it is timeless. It does not end in one lifetime unlike the other dots. When we do not believe in the concept of rebirth, then we have trouble in separating the salt (perceptive body) from the water (soul). Due to this, the invisible bodies seem inseparable from each other and realizations of the soul do not become the focus of one's spiritual journey in one lifetime. Hence, such seekers can fall into the trap of making their intellect the sole master of their decisions. This eventuality has caused resistance in the human evolution and has led to friction among religions taking away centuries of development due to lack of a long-term vision. Each generation had been focusing on its current lifetime maximization and eventually this has led to a lesser whole for all generations to come.

All the five dots and their proper wiring make up your sparkling inner cosmos. Metaphorically, you need the car, the navigator, the driver and the passenger to make the journey worthwhile. Only with the soul as the true master of the complete self, can you realize your true calling and your full potential in living your life. When you say, 'Namaste' (pronounced 'Namha-stu-te'), literally meaning 'I bow-unto-you', with folded hands and in a bowed posture, the 'I' identity here refers to the complete self—the body in posture, the emotions in gratitude, the intellect in obedience and the soul in compassion, offering homage to the other being(s). This 'I' is the true complete self. With this realization of the complete self, you have begun to awaken your soulprint.

3

SPEND TIME WITH YOUR SOUL

Spiritual strength comes when you spend time with your soul. This act is of just being and not doing anything. Due to the excessive time spent in the material world, we have sadly developed a relationship of instant gratification even with ourselves. Whatever gives us pleasure is considered to be an 'exciting' or a 'sought after' thing and whatever takes away the 'kick', is considered to be 'boring'.

The spiritual realm, however, works on a different set of principles, for here we seek balance and peace instead of instant gratifications and energy boosts. So, your expectations have to be different when you decide to spend time with your soul. In the beginning, you, the seeker, will not get any gratification and might get impatient and choose not to spend time with your soul. Be patient about your impatience! If you do not like to spend time with yourself then who will like to spend time with you? *Spending time with your soul is called meditation.*

Meditation

Meditation is an act of being. Contrary to popular belief, it is not an act of doing. During meditation, all your inner dots or identities are silent and your awareness of being is with your soul. In these hectic times, this concept of *just being* may feel alien to your system. When you meditate, your intellect is silent and no 'happy hormones' like serotonins are released, thus you may not enjoy meditation and might think of giving it up like many others do on their journey. Moreover, since you are so used to living in the world with your intellect being supreme, when it is silenced during meditation the intellect might think of ways to avoid doing it. On a positive step towards meditation first few times you may fall into a deep peaceful sleep. These sessions of sleep are the signals of you moving in the right direction of spending time with your soul. Over a period of time, sleep will turn into a half meditative sleep where your intellect is silent but your awareness is active all around your complete self.

A Million-Realization Question

A Million-Realization Question is that whether happiness is a state of being or a pleasurable act? For instance, when you sit with your loved ones, your parents or children or spouse or a friend, many a time it is just the act of *being* with them that gives you happiness and peace and not anything specifically that they have to do or say to 'make' you happy! Similarly, just being with your soul or eternal self will also give you peace and happiness, as it is truly the centre of your universe. The more time you spend with it, the more you realize of its existence and its truth.

In initial meditation sessions, the relationship starts like that of strangers meeting each other for the first time, but in no time it blossoms into the most beautiful 'friendship', as your soul is the space that has lifetimes of association with your current identity. Realizing who you truly are, inside, gives you more clarity on what you want to be or not be on the outside. The stronger the bond you have with your soul, the brighter your character is on the outside.

A beautiful relationship is like a fragrant flower, kept in a book, over a period of time. When you take one look at the book or the flower, all the memories come back instantaneously. Likewise, spending time with your eternal self comes from a timeless relationship. It keeps you at peace and happiness as in that state you are in complete balance of your *reality* (outer) and your *realizations* (inner). Realization comes from the inner depiction of what is outside, as seen by your soulprint. Time has no importance in a timeless space; so, spending time with your soul cannot be measured in terms of clock hours used. Its awakening is ascertained by the abundant realizations discovered by you on your inner journey of meditation.

Meditation through Yoga

There are many ways to connect your inner dots in unison, which are referred to as yoga by the Vedic wisdom. The word 'yoga' comes from the word 'yuj' which means 'to connect' or the 'union', in this instance, the connection of the inner dots.

Chanting AUM

One of the many ways to meditate, as per the Vedic wisdom, is by chanting of the word 'AUM' (also known as 'OM'). AUM is the universal cosmic sound. Many modern-day scientists have claimed to hear it in the Universe's vibrations. If you look at it, purely from the scientific point of view (and not through the coloured lens of any religion), then also you can feel the purity of its vibrations.

The sacred sound 'AUM' consists of *four* letters. The first letter 'A', pronounced as 'O', encapsulates the whole Universe in its round shape and sound. 'O' is significant for its 'spherical' shape of the mouth, which is aligned with the spherical reference to the cosmos and its elements and motions. On vibrating the sound 'O' from your lips you encapsulate the whole of cosmos through your intentions in your inner self. The second letter 'U', pronounced as "Uoo", is the sound where you narrow your lips from 'O', that is, narrow the Universe and tune its vibrations *unto your self*. It is like tuning the radio frequency with your inside bandwidth, in order to connect the Universe with the receiver (yourself). On vibrating, the sound 'Uooo' you connect to your navel point to the outside Universe. This is the way you connect the outer universe with your inner self. The third sound 'M', pronounced as 'Hmmm', is the sound where you close your lips and capture the Universe's tuned-in vibrations, to spread them inside your entire body and mind. At this stage, your complete self is filled with cosmic vibrations and has aligned your inner vibrations of the body with those vibrations received from the Universe in the first two sounds. No other sound known to man vibrates inside closed lips as the sound of 'Hmmm'. The fourth letter is the *blank space* created when you complete the chant of AUM and before you begin the next chant. This silence is a state of being of the Universe and is characterized by 'nothingness'. During this silent time and space, you spend time with your soul, and all your other identities are in silence. This moment of completion brings awareness of your soul in tandem with the silent existence of the Universe. The Upanishads discuss this fourth letter in great detail and gives it equal, if not more, importance than the first three.

Interestingly, when you chant 'AUM', you exhale air into the Universe and get the Universe's vibrations inside you. Symbolically, it is the offering of your life breath in exchange for the Universe's connect with your soul. At the time of your birth the soul separated from the Universe and came to life in the material world. The relationship of the body and soul started with infusing the life breath, and now in this act of chanting 'Aum' you choose to give a little of life breath back, in order to connect with the Universe albeit for a few moments. The experience and realizations of meditation is magical in its own way.

Chanting Mantras

One more way to meditate is through chanting mantras. The word, 'mantra' comes from two Sanskrit words 'manas' meaning the mind and 'trai' meaning 'to give up', that is, to free the perceptive body to discover the soul dot. The repetitive function of chanting helps to control the perceptive bodies in two ways. One is that the intellect dot, emotive dot and the body dot become tired and numb by performing the task repeatedly. As perceptive bodies do not wander, they release your awareness and in that instance, the other invisible self, that is, your soul gets your attention. This meditation activity helps you to find your eternal self.

The second way pertains to the different chants having different vibrations and meanings. The wisdom embedded in any mantra has a specific purpose and a particular kind of tuning with the cosmos. Different mantras, therefore, fill up different aspirations of your soulprint. For example, the mantra *Om Namah Shivay* encapsulates whatever you seek. It first connects you with the Universe's vibration with the chant of 'Om' and then it connects all your five inner dots in obeisance through the word 'Namah' to the Super Soul 'Shivay', as the supreme being of the spiritual and manifested world. Therefore it is a complete 'maha' mantra that helps you seek liberation towards your soulful self. There are thousands of mantras and each connects your soul with the cosmos, for seeking different realizations.

Another way to control your perceptive bodies (emotive and intellect dots) is to not feed the body sensors with any information from the surrounding environment. When there is no feed of information to the senses (body dot) from outside, and from the senses to your perceptive bodies, you become aware of your inner space, that is, to be with your soul. In this way, you 'see' or realize the truth of your soulprint just like you get to see the true colour of a liquid once you remove it from a coloured glass. When you can 'see' or experience your existence without your perceptive bodies, then you have realized a complete meditative state.

Eight Steps to a Meditative State

One of the time-tested and systematic ways to meditate has been well defined in Sage Patanjali's Yoga Sutras, called Ashtanga. Ashtanga comes from conjugation of two Sanskrit words 'Asht', meaning 'eight' and 'anga' meaning 'parts of a body', that is, eight parts of a systematic process. These eight steps beautifully and systematically take your awareness from your outer world towards the union with your inner world, the soul. Yoga is a science and like any other science, it is systematic. You cannot skip steps or take shortcuts to achieve the desired results.

The first three steps of Ashtanga Yoga are for the body dot to be at peace and to be ready for the union with the emotive dot. The next two steps are for the emotive dot to be at peace and to connect with the intellect dot. The next two steps are for the intellect dot to be at peace with itself and be ready for the union with the soul. The seventh step is to be present with the soul (meditate) and the eighth step is to be in union with the Universe along with your complete self, comprising all the five dots. These eight steps are-

1. Yama (order in the outside space),
2. Niyama (order in the body space),
3. Asana (body posture of equanimity),
4. Pranayama (breathing to connect outside with the inside),
5. Pratyahara (withdrawal of the sensory signals),

6. Dharana (focus and thoughtfulness),
7. Dhayna (meditation) and
8. Samadhi (a state of bliss).

Each step needs to be practised one at a time, to understand and realize its nature and essence; however, by following all the eight steps consecutively, you attain a complete meditative state for attaining bliss.

Yama

Yama, or the order in the outer world, is the first step in the journey to your within, which begins from the place where you are physically present. There should be order and peace in the external environment for one to not get unwanted vibrations and disturbances. If you are not comfortable in your surroundings or if there is a lot of noise, light, heat, etc. then your senses will be on high alert and your focus will be on the outside environment. Order, in the external environment, also refers to not doing any actions whose reactions will come and disturb your balance. For instance, if you steal from your neighbour, your environment will vibrate with distrust and suspicion and your awareness will be always occupied to guard you from your neighbour. Therefore, it is best to make peace with your environment and keep it in a state of equanimity. To escape the worldly vibrations, rishis of ancient times chose to go to a forest or a mountaintop to meditate. However, one can find solitude in a fish market too, if one has trained one's perceptive bodies well, and has kept peace with the surroundings.

Niyama

Niyama, which comes from the word 'niyam' or 'discipline' is the second step and endeavours to put your body systems in order. You need to be at peace with your body dot and live a disciplined and an orderly life. In a broader view, niyama also refers to following a healthy lifestyle and exercising for a fitter and coordinated body. Just as there should be no disturbance from the outside environment, there shouldn't be any disturbance from within the body, due to any short-term or long-term imbalances brought on by you in the functioning of the body's internal systems. Healthy perceptive bodies reside only in a disciplined body.

Asana(s)

Asana is the balanced posture of the body. There are different asanas for different purposes. You can choose any comfortable posture to practice meditation. One of the easiest postures for meditation is *Sukhasana,* that is, sitting in a crossed leg position by keeping your back straight, with your head, neck and back in alignment, shoulder and abdominal muscle relaxed, the hands resting on your knees, eyes closed and your body remains without motion during the practice.

Another easy posture is *Shavasana,* or the 'lying dead posture'. In this posture, you lie on your back on the floor or a mat spread on the floor, with your hands and legs equidistant from the centre of your body (any comfortable distance is fine). Each muscle of your body, starting from the toes moving up to the head, should be relaxed. Realizing this wisdom, of having a balanced posture while doing your daily work, can lead to better concentration and energy flow in your body and your work environment.

Pranayama

Pranayama is made up of two Sanskrit words: 'prana' means 'the life breath' and 'ayama' means 'to go in and out'. Life breath and soul go hand in hand and life breath cannot exist without the soul in the manifested world. When the soul departs, we can put a body on a ventilator to pump oxygen into the lungs but that is not the same as life breath, that is, the life force. Your breath is the symbiotic connection of the (your) self with the Universe, as you breathe in the air from the cosmos only to be returned for the survival of the plants. While practising Pranayama, modulating the speed and depth of your breath needs practice. The best way to breathe in deep, is to push one's navel out while breathing in. Few people mistake deep breathing with pushing their chests out, which only expands the top of the lungs and not its main sack. Pushing your navel out, while inhaling, ensures that the bags of the lungs are filled with air. When you are aware of each breath leaving your body, you will get a feeling of letting go (of something very important—your life breath). While exhaling, you experience relaxation of the muscles which were holding on to something inside and thus were strained. Through Pranayama you connect your inner identities and are aware of your inner and outer cosmos.

Pratyahara

Pratyahara consists of the words, 'pratya' meaning 'without' and 'ahara' meaning 'food', which means to not feed the body-senses and to mute all gratifications. Your five senses send signals to your brain, to process them, so that your body can act accordingly. For this reason, we usually close our eyes, ears and mouth, and put our hands in a comfortable resting position during meditation. In a broader view, Pratyahara means 'letting go'. When you let go of your attachments, likes and dislikes and other form of *psychological bondages*, your perceptive bodies free up and your physical body feels lighter. In that instance, your intellect does not harbour any attachments which leads to its liberation from all self consuming pleasures called sins namely; kama (lust), krodh (anger), lobha (greed), moha (fascination), mada (sloth) and matsarya (envy). Even fasting, for spiritual reasons, comes from the internal state of Pratyahara where the person demonstrates self-control and no desire for any indulgences.

Dharana

'Dharana', means to 'hold' or 'retain' the intellect; and to have a single-minded focus. When you pick up an object, you leave all the other objects on the table. Similarly, when you focus on only one thing then you shed the other musings of your intellect. During Dharana, apart from focusing on a thought you can also choose to concentrate on a physical point; preferably the space between your two eyebrows. By doing so, you bring all your energies to a point in your intellect dot. That 'point' could be an idea or a vision that you are holding on to in your perceptive body to evolve further. To tame your 'monkey mind' filled with disturbing and elusive thoughts, or to handle chaos in your everyday life, practising this step of yoga will give you, the seeker, greater clarity, mindfulness and focus.

Dhyana

Dhyana is the combination of two words 'dhi' meaning the 'intellect' and 'yana' meaning the 'vehicle to move' that is, to focus the intellect towards any dot, in this instance, the soul. Dhyana is a *meditative state* where you want 'to be' with your soul, which begets the question, where does the soul reside in your body? Does it reside in your intellect or head, your emotive self or your heart? A wise man once said, 'In your body, the soul resides nowhere and everywhere!' The soul is like a cloud of consciousness in and around us. In the first six steps, you have learnt how to connect the inner dots, which is *not* the same as spending time with your true self, the soul.

In this step, you understand the nature of the intellect as a wanderer and accept it. *The intellect is like the blowing wind, which can never be controlled.* All you can do is observe the wind just like a person watching the wind blowing outside through a window. When you do not give your intellect any attention or have any intention to control it, then it understands that the purpose of wandering is not its sole purpose. Most people are in the habit of taking off with their thoughts and contemplations. Focusing on your breath is like 'staying indoors'; it helps you to be uninvolved in the musings of the mind. In this step, you realize this wandering nature of the intellect and your non-responsiveness is the solution towards controlling it. Being with the soul, as an observer, and watching the intellect as an audience creates a state of peace, as you realize that you are *not* the floating mind. The soul does not have any questions and its purpose is 'to be' and just observe life's realizations. *Living life from the point of view of one's soul is called soulful living.* Observing the inner and outer worlds, without reacting to it, is the essence of meditation.

Samadhi

The word 'Sam-a-dhi' is made up of three words—'sam' means 'completely aligned', 'a' means 'near to' and 'dhi' means 'the intellect', meaning where the soul is completely aligned to the intellect, emotive self, life breath and the physical body as one complete whole. Like a tree is connected to the soil, your complete self is connected to the Universe through your soul. The Sanskrit term, '*Aham Brahmasmi!*' means, 'I am Brahman' and encapsulates the thought of your oneness with the Universe and refers to the state of complete self-realization.

Your intellect, emotive and the body dot along with the breath, led by your soul, becomes the central force of your existence. They get trained to not float around in the vast Universe while performing the Ashtanga Asanas. The deeper and slower you breathe, the closer you are to the self, as the outside air and your inside breath exchanges seamlessly. When you are too busy, stressed or contemplating on difficult issues, your breathing becomes shallow and shows your disconnect with the outer world. This makes your mind and body suffer in the form of pain, headache, migraine, etc. due to lack of oxygen supply to your muscles, which become constricted in the process. Hence, your life breath is connected with the working of your inner dots in more ways than you know and simply focusing on your breath, especially during tough situations, helps you to concentrate better and alleviate many of your inner challenges in order to solve the outer ones.

Yoga of the Mind

By practising yoga, you learn to spend quality time with your soulprint. At an advanced stage, with increased experience, you will be soulful all the time. You carry on with your everyday chores while being in a meditative state. The goal of being on a spiritual path is to continue with your daily life, while being continuously soulful. Making your work focus on soulfulness and in making your soul present in your work is the centre of any work-life balance. When your inner soulful relationship is at peace, then all your external relationships become happier and peaceful. For a right or happy relationship it is not only important *to find* the right and happy person, but also *to be* the right and happy person! When you are happy to spend time with yourself, then everyone around you will also like to hang out with you!

The active voice of your soul is silence. When you have nothingness present inside you then you are ready to seek and grow. As we cannot add water to a glass full of water, similarly only when your soul is in a state of emptiness and silence, you can add more spiritual wisdom to it, through realizations.

After building a strong soulful state, the next step in your journey is to realize its limitless potential. Without connecting all the inner dots well, your self-realization becomes very limited. In a starry night, it is up to you to connect the dots (or stars) to make your own constellations out of them. You need to be aware of the existence and of the connections or the relationships of your inner dots. This will make your energy flow smooth and, in turn, make you illumined to shine the light in your universe of friends and family and other fellow travellers.

4

UNDERSTAND THE LEVELS OF YOUR CONSCIOUSNESS

Each planet in the Solar System is an active multidimensional system of energy. Likewise, each of your inner dots forms a multidimensional sphere or shell (also called sheath), which not only has unique characteristics but also interacts with others shells in its own way. It is important to understand the energies of these inner spheres to keep them aligned and interactive. A wise man once said, 'If two people agree all the time then one of them is useless. If they disagree all the time then both of them are useless!' Similarly, all your inner dots need to be interactive as much as aligned, with each other, in keeping their presence active. Just like a symphony, all the sheaths need to harmonize to create your own music of life.

Levels of Consciousness

The inner universe, as explained in the Taittiriya Upanishad, includes five bodies or sheaths also called kosha or levels of consciousness. Vedic wisdom, has laid out that you need to be aware of these five spiritual sheaths or levels and this awareness is the first step. You are already living each moment in your life from the perspective of one of these five bodies or their combinations thereof. Now is the time to just become aware of what you do. All five sheaths namely, the body, the life breath, the emotive, the intellect and the soul, have their own centre of focus and purpose of existence. Interestingly, all the five centres are aligned like a spiral. When you move from the centre of lower sheaths to the higher ones, you can stay aligned with each one simultaneously.

All the five sheaths or levels carry out important functions that are required for a complete life experience. However, living life out of the body sheath is a 'lower experiential life' whereas living life at the level of soul sheath is 'higher experiential life'. The quest of your spiritual journey is to move from one level of existence, that is, the 'lower level' towards the 'higher or deeper levels'. Humans are the luckiest species as they have the most evolved spiritual wisdom and can live from perspective of any sheath. Therefore, *soulful living is a matter of choice* of the depth of awareness that the seeker chooses to live a full life.

Primary Elements

Coincidental, to the five inner sheaths the physical outer world is also made up of five primary elements. Everything is a combination of these five essential elements and can be reduced to these five elements. Hence these elements are called the purest building blocks of the material cosmos. Each element has peculiar characteristics to itself. These five elements are earth (matter), water, air, fire and ether (or space).

Earth (as matter) refers to the physical materials present in the cosmos. 'Matter' has the characteristics of solidity, and is three-dimensional and is kept as an inert weighing object in the cosmos and is governed by the gravitational pull of earth.

Water is in a liquid state and is formless in nature and it takes the form of the vessel it is put into. It is flexible as it changes from being in a liquid, gaseous or solid state, depending upon the temperature it is put under. Water flows downwards and always tries to maintain balance between two of its interconnected levels.

Air is in the gaseous state, which has characteristic of being invisible and floats in the cosmos. It moves free of gravity and flows in every possible direction. It is expandable and fills up any space provided.

Fire is the fourth element and is in the form of active heat and its energy usually flows upwards. Fire, itself does not change form but is used to transform one element into another, like water into steam (air). Fire helps to differentiate all physical elements through the process of fractionalization.

Ether also referred to as 'sky' or spirit and is spatial in characteristic. It is omnipresent and omniscient in the cosmos. It does not move in any direction and is simply just present. It is present in the environment in the form of the sky and the Universe and also in-between Nano particles of matter. The nature of ether is to just exist (to be) and is very peculiar as there is no sense of direction or sense of time about it.

Spiritual Connect To The Material World

Level 1–The Body Sheath

The body sheath is also called the 'Annamaya Kosh' and refers to the physical body dot, which as per the Upanishads is made up of 'anna' or food. In essence, this refers to the primal element *earth* as described above. Food makes your physical body, which is bound by physical dimensions, and all the laws applicable to matter, that is, of solidity in the form of shape and size that defines its structure. During yama, niyama and asana, you 'are at' the centre of the physical body awareness. All non-life forms like rocks, wood are present only at this level of existence. This body sheath includes all the soft attributes like your name, goodwill, relationships and the hard attributes like your wealth and assets that constitute your material world. The body sheath answers the existential question of *whom* in our life. When you say, 'I am doing the act' or this is 'my son', it is in connotation to your body dot. It is also instrumental in physically changing your external environment. The expiry of this sheath is the fastest among all sheaths as material (things) and parts of human body wither during a lifetime.

Level 2–The Life Breath Sheath

The life breath sheath is also called the 'Pranamaya Kosh' with its centre of awareness present in your central breathing organ, the lungs. When you breathe, the air percolates to a central point inside you. It is here that the breath is exchanged with your inside life breath. Without 'prana' or life breath there is no life. All life forms like grass, plants etc. exist at this level of awareness. This sheath is like the invisible backbone of your other four inner bodies, giving them structure and formation through your awareness. During Pranayama, you can choose to connect with all the other dots of the inner and outer self by being aware of their existence. Unlike the physical body, life breath has more dimensions and expanse. In essence, this sheath refers to the *element air* and answers the question of *where* in our existence. For instance, air is present everywhere but air pressures help air to circulate. Likewise, your life breath is present everywhere in your body but takes your awareness to different parts of your body and levels of consciousness depending upon pressures that build in them. This sheath expires at the end of your lifetime as life breath and life go hand in hand, and one cannot exist without the other. Unlike the body sheath and its accumulation, this sheath cannot be stolen, destroyed or transferred during your life.

Level 3–The Emotive Sheath

The emotive sheath or the 'Manomaya Kosh' has its centre of awareness in your feelings and emotions. This sheath exists like *element water* in your body and answers the existential question of *what* in our life. For instance, questions ranging from *what* colour you should wear, to *what* characteristic of a life partner you would want are topics of emotive sheath to ponder! Emotive sheath helps you to choose. It is closely associated with your heart, as your blood flow is influenced by your emotions. In essence, your *feelings* and *emotions* have the same characteristic as that of the element water. Emotions are fluid and can change from flexibility to solidity to non-existence, as their surrounding environment easily influences them. This awareness is realized through the meditative step of the 'Pratyahara', where you mute all your senses and detach yourself in order to control your ripple-like impulses. This emotive sheath is present in all living forms that have advanced sensory organs like animals. The expiry (scope) of this sheath is more than one lifetime as your relationships and emotive connects exist as long as people connected to you are alive, even after you are gone.

Level 4–The Intellect Sheath

The intellect sheath is also called 'Gyaanmaya Kosh' and centre of its awareness lies in your brain. Its nature is similar to the *element fire* and answers the question of *how* of your existence. For instance, *how* do you do your work, or *how much* time do you put into a project, etc. Your intellect helps you to measure and find the most effective and efficient balance in carrying out your work. The intellect's role is to contemplate, add, subtract, divide, multiply and then decide. From these characteristics, comes the concept of *Agni Pareeksha* meaning to ascertain the truth of a matter or a substance. This awareness is practised in the meditative step of Dharna (focus). You can understand, analyse and create the material world only through your intellect. The expiry (scope) of this sheath is many lifetimes as your wealth and creations can last for centuries but not forever.

Level 5–The Soul Sheath

The soul sheath is also called the 'Anandmaya Kosh' and the centre of its awareness lies in your soul (or atma). As per Hindu belief, the soul's centre is in the 'atmaram bone', which is present in the ribcage closest to the heart. However, the soul is a cloud of consciousness and engulfs our existence completely. It is a state of pure spiritual wisdom and answers the existential question of *why* in your life. Your purpose for doing anything or your goals in this lifetime are rooted in the question, 'why do you want to do this?' This ostensibly answers your current goals, however, usually your activies are based on the true callings of your life. The true purpose of your life might be dormant and awaiting your awakening, but it is the hidden wisdom to all the whys or purposes that you put forth in your everyday living. Its nature is like the *element ether*, encapsulating emptiness and a state of just being. This awareness is practised in the meditative step of 'Dhyana' (or meditation). The soul like ether does not move or flow in any direction. The soul is timeless, limitless and all pervasive. The soul has no expiry as it gets transferred from this lifetime to the next, till *eternity*.

Living a Complete Life

All the sheaths work in unison to form a complete human existence. The purpose of your spiritual and material existence is to be one complete independent unit. This is similar to the combination of the five primary elements working in unison and forming an independent complete unit called the earth. In the meditative step of Samadhi, you practise being aware of your five inner dots as one. At that complete higher level of consciousness, you connect with the higher energy level of the Super Soul, which answers the existential questions of *when* of your life. For instance, *when* you choose to awaken your soulprint, then you start to be in unison with all your elements and you float freely with the cosmic energy. This realization of the natural flow of your energies is the basis of eternal evolution that you experience over lifetimes. Hence, it is only a matter of time as to 'when', you will awaken to a higher state. Perhaps in this lifetime or the next or many lifetimes forth, but you will get what your soulprint truly seeks. Existing as a complete interconnected self is the ultimate goal of your journey to self-realization.

Path of Soulful Living

As you move from the material or physical world to the spiritual world, you simultaneously move from the body sheath to a soulful sheath. Each successive level of awareness is higher and goes deeper into your inner self. *The deeper you go inside, the higher and wider you go outside.* You choose to spend your time on the chosen level of your existence depending upon the present expanse of realizations of your soulprint. Your current *spiritual quotient or consciousness* defines which sheath you spend most of your time in, that is, a state of comfort (body sheath) *or* maximization of your desires (emotive sheath) *or* a state of self-gratification (intellect sheath) *or* a state of compassion and universal alignment (soulful sheath). Even as a human, you might choose to live at a lower level of awareness, fulfilling only your bodily desires instead of soulful existence, and there is nothing wrong about that as it is all part of your evolutionary process. To think and also propagate the thought for others that your level is 'the best level to be at' is not the best way ahead in anyone's journey. However, a deeper level of awareness imbibes a broader vision of the cosmos and a space for everyone to co-exists. For instance the enlightened leaders in human history gave up their personal life and chose to live at higher levels by doing soulful actions for the greater good, thereby realizing a higher life experience.

Maslow's Theory

Abraham Maslow, in his 1943 paper, 'A Theory of Human Motivation', proposed a theory in psychology. Maslow's theory on human behaviour, in essence, connects the inner sheaths with human behaviours. Maslow's hierarchy of needs, represented as a pyramid, consists of five levels namely physical or physiological needs, safety and security needs, social needs, self-esteem needs and self-actualization needs. Each of these needs corresponds to the central focus of the five inner sheaths: The physical needs for the body sheath, the security needs for the life breath sheath, the social needs for the emotive sheath, the self-esteem needs for the intellect sheath and the self-actualization needs for the soul sheath.

Thus, your outer goals and motivations are reflected in your inner universe and vice versa. In this way, you find the eastern spirituality is deeply connected with the western science of human behaviour. For instance, in a corporate structure, the frontline workers are compensated for their physical activity in the form of daily wages (body sheath). As we move up the corporate ladder, the compensation to the next levels of workers is given more for their time and leadership qualities (emotive and intellectual sheath) instead of their actual measurable physical activity. At the top of the company, the chairman is expected to provide a vision for the whole organization to experience (soulful sheath). A prudent vision needs to be closely aligned with the outer environment, both commercially and socially and hence deemed to be soulful.

As you progress professionally, your position in the organization (body sheath) and your level of consciousness (soulful sheath) have to move in tandem. Each level of existence is important, as it's a part of the organizational hierarchy. However, when you graduate to a higher level, in your outside (corporate world) or inside (spiritual world), it is imperative to ensure that no imbalance exists between your two worlds and you need to work on both the worlds, simultaneously. This is the imbalance that causes the beautiful trees to fall. In essence this is the foundation of all your life choices as well as your successful and happy career!

Happy Hormones

Interestingly, even the body's biochemistry corresponds with these five sheaths at the molecular level. The endocrine system secretes many happy hormones most prominently Endorphins, Adrenaline, Oxytocin, Dopamine and Serotonin (or Melatonin). All these chemicals can be naturally boosted in your living by two main activities of your body—*exercise (external space) and meditation (inner space)*. Happy hormones also work in combination with each other for an overall well being of the body and attain the 5Cs—comfort, control, contentment, concentration and compassion for your holistic life experience.

Endorphins

Endorphins are secreted by the pituitary gland to meet extra energy requirements such as exercise, childbirth, etc. This hormone kicks in when you are in the body sheath perspective of awareness. By secretion of this hormone, your body does not feel as much pain due to the extra physical activity and brings a feeling of balance in form of *comfort* in your living.

Adrenaline

Adrenaline is secreted by the adrenaline glands and provides extra impetus to your respiratory system on account of fight or flight response activities carried on by your body. As your respiratory system overworks, your breathing increases by the secretion of this hormone, which gives extra energy to your muscles. This balances your need to act with more energy and gives you a feeling of control for your safety and security in your life breath sheath perspective of awareness.

Oxytocin

Oxytocin is a happy hormone that is secreted by the pituitary gland in your brain when you emotionally bond with others. This hormone is active when you are in the emotive sheath perspective of awareness. This hormone is essential as it gives you *contentment* when you fulfil your need for social interactions.

Dopamine

Dopamine is secreted by the hypothalamus part of your brain. It plays a role in how you feel pleasure. It is a big part of the unique human ability to think and plan. Dopamine helps your brain to *concentrate* to maximize your pleasure. This hormone is active when you are in the intellect sheath perspective of awareness.

Serotonin

Serotonin is secreted by the pineal gland in your brain when you feel *compassion* or empathy for others. This hormone is active when you are in the spiritual sheath perspective of awareness. In your act of helping others and doing greater good for the society, this happy hormone helps you reach a state of happiness and peace in your actions based out of your *compassion.*

Staircase to Higher Living

All this spiritual wisdom might make you want to ask a Million-Realization Question—should you live at the highest level of your consciousness?

All the inner dots when well connected form the complete self. All the levels are important and your awareness keeps shifting among the levels as you live your daily life. *Each soulprint will choose its level of existence at a given time, based on its own set of experiences and realizations.* For instance, a few soulprints live only for themselves, others live for their family, while some choose to live for their community, country or even the world. If you try to be soulful (higher) without first balancing your other (lower) dots, then you will fall back to your actual level due to the ignorance of those dots. All levels are important and are stepping stones for the higher path. As you awaken in your inner journey, you will spend more time first balancing your body dot, then your perceptive bodies and eventually your spiritual sheath. An awakened soulprint is present while taking its everyday life decisions, and this is the way for soulful living.

5

YOUR JOURNEY TO PEACE, HAPPINESS AND BLISS

Everyone wants to find peace and happiness in their lives and yet both remain the most elusive. The reason is that *they are simply not a 'thing' or a gratification that can be 'gotten'.* Peace, happiness and bliss are different experiences of the state of inner being. You may have experienced one state or another, that too once in a while but have not been able to stay there perpetually. Attaining a *perpetual state of peace and happiness* has been the Holy Grail for seekers since time immemorial. Each soulprint, as per its level of consciousness, has its own expectation of what peace and happiness mean and mostly confuse them with pleasures and gratifications of the senses. Each of your inner dots behaves in a peculiar way and is connected with the other dots uniquely. Each of the five bodies of your inner universe contributes towards your experiencing these different states of spiritual providence. When you are able to take your level of consciousness to the higher state of inner balance of your five dots, and maintain your state of being at that level, you experience a state of perpetual peace and perfect happiness, which is a blissful state.

Your Journey to Happiness

A state of happiness already exists around you. Nature is abundant and hence in a state of happiness. In essence, when you realize that *you are abundant* you experience happiness. Then you see happiness in everything around you and spend more time enjoying nature and its abundance. *Being abundant* is different from *gathering abundance*, for one is an inner state of being and the other is an outer measure of wealth. The journey to happiness is an internal one and starts from understanding the flow of the energies of your five inner dots and the wisdom in connecting them to attain a happy state.

Balance Your Body

The physical body is a 'biological machine' that consumes energy to survive and in return also gives energy back to the ecosystem. It works on the law of physics, that no energy is ever destroyed or lost but simply changes form from one to the other. The body dot is made up of and interacts with the five primal elements namely air, water, earth, ether and fire. To this extent whatever input (food, water and air) we add into the body system, the same gets used, stored or returned to the cosmos by the body dot. Flow of energy from each dot affects the other dots and in turn also gets affected by its own behaviour.

Just as the ecosystem works at a macro level, the human body works at the micro level, that is, the body strives to attain discipline and order (niyam) in its working. It uses body senses like touch, sight, smell, hearing and taste to carry on its functioning. All its actions along with other internal body systems like the digestive system, circulatory system, immune system, urinary system, work in an organized balanced way.

On smooth functioning of the body dot, where you consume equivalent to what you give back, you experience a state of comfort in your life. When you consume any one element (say) food in excess, then your body dot tries to accommodate and digest and even store this extra energy for later use. However, stressing this accommodation of the body to its limits, imbalances it in the form of diseases like obesity, kidney and lung problems, and blood pressure. Mostly due to reasons of excessive or poor inputs in way of unhealthy lifestyle (emotive choices), the body experiences uneasiness or handicaps, which inhibit it in carrying out its functions and thus lowers your life experiences.

Diminishing Returns Imbalances You

The body dot is a subset of the emotive dot. Through the body's five senses, the emotive dot interacts with the body and experiences pleasures or gratifications. For example, when you eat food that tastes good you feel good and eat more. This gratification of desire to eat more when connected with the intellect, works towards enhancing your pleasures. In this way, your inner dots tries to maximize and make up most of the sensory pleasures. Thus, your intellect measures 'how much' you felt and basis its expectations on 'how much you want more' to feel more gratified. Your feelings start to become measurable goals and when you 'achieve' more of that invisible target, then you feel successful and when you achieve less you feel as if you have failed. This blind chase or way of life towards pleasure maximization becomes a never-ending cycle. However, this feeling of fullness is temporary as the when cause of gratification is removed, your pleasurable experience also ceases. Further, with every 'kick' you get from such consumption, your expectations increase; and the magnitude of the 'kick' (return) diminishes with additional intakes due to the law of diminishing returns. Thus, with initial consumption you feel the high but with successive consumption, the feeling reduces. Hence, in the hope of maximizing pleasures you always end up feeling unsatisfied and disappointed, as your expectations to feel-good increases but your actual feel good experiences decreases. This gap between expectation and experience results in the imbalance of your emotive state. Your every 'successful' or 'unsuccessful' action dominoes into higher imbalances (of your intellect) by causing psychological disorders like depression, anxiety and stress.

The Wisdom of Holistic Wellness

The work of the intellect is to maximize pleasure and this gets complicated when one dot works unilaterally without paying attention to the others. For example, your emotive dot might crave for a cigarette, which is not a physically healthy choice to make. The intellect, in such a scenario, can only satisfy one dot and can choose to overrule the other. For instance, in the case of smoking, either the emotive or the body dot can be balanced but not both. Similarly, satisfying the desires to excessively eat or drink can unbalance both the dots, due to a subsequent feeling of guilt felt by your emotive self. Other misplaced longings of the emotive dot, say, the desire to be slim and hence 'beautiful' can further devoid the body system of the basic nutrition and can result in low energy levels. Such imbalances are created due to non-alignment or friction of dots among themselves. The intellect, in essence, has to analyse different impulses and rationalize, in order to work towards the holistic wellness of the self. Thus, inner and intra balancing of all dots is a continuous goal of the intellect. Keeping your emotive dot in a state of satisfaction (energized) and at the same time keeping your body dot in a state of comfort (ready to perform) and your life breath dot in a state of calmness (alertness to perform) is the balance sought by the intellect through focus and mindfulness in a quest to attain holistic wellness.

Seek Happiness, Not Pleasures

It is common for seekers to confuse pleasure with happiness. Simply put, you are happy when you feel abundant with respect to your expectations or your desires. Though both pleasure and happiness are experienced in the emotive state yet they are very different from each other. Pleasures are experiences out of the body dot whereas happiness is the state of the perceptive dots. Pleasures focus on sensory gratifications whereas happiness is a state of being, where you realize that you have more than what you need or desire. Pleasures are temporary as when any of the body senses stop consuming, the pleasures cease. Happiness lasts longer as you can be mindful of the state of being happy as long as you choose. Pleasures can be bought in the marketplace as it pertains to the body dot, whereas happiness is a state of mind and cannot be transferred. Pleasures never accrue to the soul dot, whereas happiness can be connected to the soul and can be taken to a higher experience. In essence, happiness is a higher living experience than pleasure, as your interactions move from an external space to an internal one.

Unravel The Secret To Happiness and Success

Seekers sometimes wrongly connect happiness with success. *Success is getting what you want but happiness is liking what you get.* Success is an experience of the intellect dot where the intellect, based on its knowledge (or ignorance!), sets goals for itself to achieve which are usually measurable and communicable in the external environment. When the person achieves, or surpasses, these goals then the person deems himself to be successful. When these *arbitrary self-goals* are not met, then the person considers himself a failure.

Happiness on the other hand is experienced irrespective of your performance or goals set by you. Success exists in the context of the outer world whereas happiness relates to the inner world. Success can be quantified whereas happiness cannot be. A million-realization learning is that happiness has been always more important than success as it enriches your life's experiences more beautifully. For instance, when a student sets *a* target and *expects* to get 90 per cent marks in an exam but gets 75 per cent then she feels 'unsuccessful'. When a student sets the target and *desires* to get 90 per cent marks but gets 75 per cent then she feels disappointed. This is how an expectation unknowingly intertwines with your desire. However, when a student only *desires to do her best* and then works hard towards the target of 90 per cent (without any expectation), she focuses on her inner energy. With this thought in mind, despite being unsuccessful in achieving her target she will feel good about putting in her best effort.

You feel contented with your performance by doing the best you can as long as you do not connect your desires with your expectations. This is similar to the desire of making a balloon big by blowing air into it. Each balloon has its own capacity to attain its maximum size. Thus, when you focus on making it a big balloon you feel happy with whatever you achieve. On the other hand, when you set your expectations to make it the *biggest* balloon as compared to the other balloons, then no matter how big the balloon gets, you will feel happy only by comparing it with other balloons. Moreover, in this *rat race* with other balloons your focus shifts away from your balloon's inner strength or its maximum capacity, and towards the achievements (sizes) of the other balloons. This misplaced focus might force you to either fill extra air into your balloon, albeit the balloon might bursts or perhaps not fill enough air as per the balloon's full capacity.

This is the mistake we see in our Indian education system of ranking students based on their marks. The students, under this uni-dimensional system of assessment, are forced to focus on the outside environment and thus falter under excessive peer pressure for no fault of theirs. This ranking system is different from evolved grading systems as seen in some countries, where they focus on multidimensional assessment, rather than only grades, as a measure of one's calibre. *When you accept that each soulprint is different then there should not be any comparison or competition*. Performing to *your fullest* should be the focus of your energy flows. Thus, a happy state is not dependent upon your success or failure but on your desires and expectations that you set for yourself to attain happiness. You can choose to work harder for your higher goals for success, and at the same time choose to be happy even in your 'failures' by considering them experiments for your learning. This is the way forward for a spiritually successful *and* a happy life.

Attaining Perfect Happiness

When you are happy and also aligned with your soul dot, your experience enhances to a higher state of being, called *perfect happiness or joy.* This means that you are happy with your inner self and at the same time compassionate and merciful to others, that is, your outer self. For instance, a sportsperson's happiness on winning a match for his country (alignment with a bigger cause) is at a higher state as compared to his state of happiness on winning just for himself. *Perfect happiness* is connected to your soulful intentions of compassion and therefore lasts longer than the feeling of happiness.

Your Journey to Being Peaceful

Apart from happiness and perfect happiness, the other important experience towards attaining bliss is a peaceful state. Peace is an experience where there is perfect balance within and among the inner dots. Like a house of cards, when each of your inner energies are in perfect balance within itself and, with others then you are in a state of peace.

Stay Calm and Be Aware

The body dot attains balance in eating (consuming), digesting (harnessing) and channelling (distributing) energy in a disciplinary and orderly way. When there is no imbalance in any of the systems working inside, you feel a *state of comfort*. In this balanced state, all systems work harmoniously and interact with other inner systems without any friction. Such a body dot is the essence of healthy living.

Similarly, the life breath dot, through its awareness maintains a sense of balance, protecting from anything that might cause imbalance to any of the inner dots. Awareness has a peculiar nature of being multidimensional and can be present at multiple places at the same time. Just like the element air, the purpose of life breath is to maintain equal inner 'atmospheric pressure' of calmness among the dots. The life breath dot on sensing imbalance, alerts the inner dots to a state of equanimity, preventing them from getting unbalanced and hence inner poise is maintained. The awareness of this perpetual balance gives a feeling of calmness to the complete self.

Stay Content and Be Mindful

The emotive dot is the most difficult to balance, as like the element water, it easily gets influenced by its environment. The emotive body creates desires which leads to positive or negative emotions in you. For instance, negative emotions such as disappointment, depression, fear, anger, disgust etc. are felt when you perceive that your reality (material world) is less than what you desired. When you feel such emotions, the emotive dot with its connect with the heart, doesn't pump blood and you feel low on energy. On the other hand, you feel elated with positive perception of the reality vis-a-vis your desires and you feel high on energy. However, these energy fluctuations by themselves are not helpful in maintaining a stable system. Thus, both the positive and negative forces further cause imbalances in the body dot and you experience anxiety, high blood pressure, irregularities in sugar (insulin) levels and so on.

The way to keep the emotive dot balanced is to keep it like still water, not soda water. This means that you need to be mindful of your desires and not connect them directly with your body systems. Also, you need to insulate your emotive dot from the external influences that might 'heat up' and lead to spilling over of your emotions. *Rich is a man with no needs.* Choose to stay content. Contentment is a state of balance of the emotive dot and is achieved when you choose to keep your desires satiated. When you are content then your intellect concentrates your energies on the balancing of the other dots. Then the intellect works towards a positive flow of energy to attain inner poise and a peaceful state. Being peaceful is thus an active state of balancing the intellect and the emotive continuously and is not a passive state.

The soul dot is always in a peaceful state of being. It sits quietly in the backseat of the 'car' while the car drives to various places. Along with the soul, when all the four dots are in a state of balance such as the body is in comfort, the life breath is calm, the emotive dot is content and the intellect dot is mindful, a complete peaceful state is experienced by you. *When you realize the truth about the nature of the inner dots and continuously choose to keep them balanced, you attain inner peace.*

Holistic Approach To a Healthy Body

While living a peaceful and happy life, if you find yourself overweight or an imbalance in the body dot and are not able to easily carry on your daily activities because of it, then each dot will take on the responsibility to strive balancing this imbalance, that is, reducing your physical weight. For instance, the emotive dot will contribute by staying contented in feeling less hunger. Moreover it will be in a positive state and release energy to assist your body dot to carry on with physical exercises. Likewise, the body dot will perform the exercises to lose the physical weight, while the intellect dot will focus on the best (most effective and efficient) exercises for the body dot. Intellect will further ascertain which healthy diet you must follow and your emotive dot will choose to stay happy with your new diet. Your life breath will keep you calm and keep you aware of your progress towards correcting this imbalance. Hence, a holistic approach is initiated for the weight loss programme where all inner dots work together to attain balance on your spiritual journey to attain peace and happiness.

Choose to be Blissful

When you are *at peace and have a feeling of perfect happiness or joy, you, the seeker, attain a blissful state.* Blissful state is a state of inner being and can be experienced even while you carry on with your everyday life. In this state, all the inner dots stay at peace and continuously evolve towards creating a higher life experience for your soulprint.

You have to consciously choose to be blissful. When unknowingly you choose otherwise or knowingly you are in a state of *bliss denial* then no one can put you in a blissful space. Thus, being blissful is completely your responsibility and gives you, the seeker, complete authority over all the inner bodies. All soulprints need to walk on the path themselves to attain it. No matter how rich, famous or resourceful you are, you will have to learn this inner management for yourself. No one else can do that job for you. A trainer or a life coach or a guru can only guide and provide you with the requisite wisdom. The 'spiritual exercises' are useful only if you choose to practise them yourself. The more you practise, the easier it becomes for you. If you take your blissful state for granted, then imbalances will creep back into your life, just like weight gain for some people. Thus, *you have to be aware of constantly balancing all your inner dots, so that the state of balance is continuously maintained at all times.*

Attaining Param Ananda - Pure Bliss

The soul dot is the master of the intellect dot, which is the master of the emotive dot, which in turn directs the body dot. When you carry out an action then who is the real 'doer' of the action—the body or the emotion or the intellect or the soul? An act in itself is not as important as the purpose that it sets out to fulfil. While imbibing the concept of soulful living, your actions should not be based out of any of the dots except the soulful ones. For instance, two people can either have sex or make love and the act may seem the same in both instances. However, the two intentions are different: the former satisfies the body's need, while the latter ensures a complete union of one complete self with the other, in a state of complete surrender.

When you connect your actions to your soul, you seek a greater purpose, which translates into goodness for all. In such an instance, all your inner bodies, including your intellect, are aligned to think and act for the benefit of everyone. Your intellect connects with other souls in the same manner it connects with your own soul because in essence all souls are part of one Super Soul. In this spiritual affinity, you trade pain and pleasure for peace and happiness, for not only yourself but for the whole ecosystem. As you carry on with your soulful acts and do not get unbalanced or attached to your ego, your energy completely connects to the soul, which is your limitless life force in the first place.

When you awaken your soulprint and wire your inner dots to simultaneously attain peace and perfect happiness, you attain a state of bliss. However, when your align your blissful state completely in sync with the workings of the ecosystem then you realize a complete state of *param ananda or pure bliss.* In this state, the soul envisions, the intellect contemplates, the emotive self gives it energy, the life breath protects, the body strives and the Universe blesses your endeavours. This journey, from living at lower levels of consciousness of feeling bodily pleasures, to moving to higher states of happiness, peace and perfect happiness, and eventually to experiencing highest state of bliss and pure bliss, is the beautiful path illumined by soulful living for any seeker.

The Truth of Karma Yoga

What is the Vedic science behind practising equanimity and harmony of the inner dots in our everyday life? In the Bhagawad Gita, Lord Krishna illustrates how to deal with the inner body dots while carrying on with your daily duties. Through his discourse on Karma Yoga, he describes the *science of connection* of the body dot, the emotive dot and the intellectual dot with the soul dot (consciousness) and the same is illustrated below:

> *karmany evadhikaras te, ma phalesu kadachana*
> *ma karma-phala-hetur bhur, ma te sango 'stv akarmani*
>
> (You are entitled to perform your duties, but do not have right to desire the fruits of your labour. You do not have the right to expect the results of your actions, and you do not have the right to your inaction.)
>
> Bhagwad Gita, Chapter 2, Verse 47

The verse beautifully describes the science behind the relationships of the inner dots and their connection. There are four parts to the verse quoted and each part relates to the role and responsibility of an inner dot.

Do Your Duty

The first part '*karmany evadhikaras te*' relates to the body dot and states that every soulprint's body has to perform duties and functions. All the actions towards everyday living, for example, even going to the office or college, are considered soulful acts of the being. The body has the right and the responsibility to carry all the acts that the complete self directs it to perform. Body dot's role is that of a follower within your complete self.

Have No Attachment to Desire

The second part of the verse '*ma phalesu kadachana*' states that you do not have the *right to desire* the fruits of your actions. This refers to your *emotive self* as it refers to your desires. In other words, do not have desires or attach yourself to the results of your actions because the actions are carried out by the body dot as its duty. The body dot's purpose of performing its duty ends with the performance of the duty itself, and should not be connected with the emotive dot to create desires for its fruits from such actions. It is easy and common to fall into the trap of focusing on the results rather than the intentions of one's actions.

Have No Expectations for Your Actions

The third part of the verse '*ma karma-phala-hetur bhur*' states that you should not have *the expectations* for the fruits of your actions. Here, it refers to the *intellect dot* as, the intellect starts to conjure future courses even before the current ones are completed. When your intellect starts to expect results of its actions, it enhances your desires. You start to equate more success with more happiness. Moreover, *expectations* presume your body to be the sole doer of such actions. You develop an ego or the belief that you are the creator of the results of your actions. When you attach your self to the expectation of the fruits of your actions, you feed your ego and connect your success to your individual efforts. You negate the possibilities that outcome of your actions can be a function of many different forces in your environment working in your favour.

We need to remind our self that the results of our actions are attributed to the cosmic energy flow along with our efforts. Hence, our inner dots alone are not responsible for the results we get in the material world. *We make our destiny but should not get attached to realizing it.* We should always be in an inner state of peace and happiness, which comes from the belief that the outer cosmic forces, though not in our control, are moving for the betterment of all individuals. We need to respect it's working and therefore be grateful for both the successes and the failures we encounter on our journey.

Thus, expectations create an imbalance as you rely only on your intellect dot. The intellect becomes a self-focused system of creating expectations and fulfilling them. Conjuring pleasures and fulfilling them for yourself is a bottomless pit. This abysmal never-ending relationship of actions seeking pleasure, resulting in further actions seeking more pleasure, deludes the intellect. This delusion leads to confusion, which in turn leads to loss of intelligence. This makes all actions focused only towards intellect dot with disregard to a holistic approach. This mental fog leads to complete imbalance thereby negating any chances of a blissful state in your life.

Renunciate But Don't Be Inactive

The final part of the verse '*ma te sango 'stv akarmani*' further clarifies that you should not get attached to inaction or not doing your duties. When your emotive and intellectual self are not 'getting' any energy or ego boost in the form of gratification or self-glorification, you tend to feel loss of energy and think that it is best to not do any work. At this time, you need to act from a deeper soulful perspective with the wisdom that not doing any actions is not the same as not getting attached to the fruits of the actions. When you act, irrespective of the outcome, you take each action as learning and increase your realizations and your soulprint evolves. An idle body is in a state of lethargy, which is contrary to the evolving nature of the cosmos. The Super Soul is evolving and the cosmos is constantly moving, so if you were to stay put then it is regressive to your spiritual growth. *Renunciation of attachment to an action is not the same as inaction.*

A Million-Realization Learning

Once Monk Kabir was meditating under the banyan tree. As he was meditating, he realized that he had an ardent desire to be a rich merchant with enormous wealth in his next life. As he meditated further, he saw himself as a wealthy merchant with all the luxuries, as he had desired. As a merchant, he was constantly negotiating with people to make financial gains. And he soon realized that being a prosperous merchant was a very unhappy state to be in because people were resorting to all kinds of self-centered negotiation tactics in reciprocation. This left him angry and disappointed. Monk Kabir finally realized that wealth has nothing to do with one's peace and happiness. As he meditated further, he realized that fame, beauty, intelligence, power, etc., had nothing to do with being blissful. When he opened his eyes, he was content being a monk and felt blissful, filled with abundance of joy and satisfaction, as he did not have any desires except the soulful ones.

You are born in this world with some characteristics but you should not get attached to them thinking they are your own. You should also, not identify yourself with those attributes that the external environment bestows upon you. These attributes could be you being rich, beautiful, intelligent, strong and so on. You might acquire or lose any of these external attributes in your lifetime as their role is only for you to experience all facets of reality. You must try to remain unattached to such features (resultants). These features that you have, or miss not having, are neither part of your identity nor required to live a fulfilling life. These attributes come from the external environment and can be taken away just as easily. A wise man once said, 'This too shall pass' to every favourable or unfavourable situation he experienced, thereby maintaining a perpetual balanced state. You should always be in a state of equanimity and peace and create your own path irrespective of your external reality at any given point in time. When you unattach yourself to the fruits that nature gives you at the start of your life, or during your lifetime, you transcend the vagaries of the material world. You will be able to 'see' beyond your circumstances and you gain greater insights into your life, which leads you to an all-encompassing vision for attaining a blissful state for yourself.

6

THE WISDOM OF THE GITA

Modern life challenges come from disconnect between the material world and the spiritual world. The material world, being external, can be seen and hence thought to be real, whereas the spiritual world, being imperceptible, is thought to be unreal. This makes us believe in the truth of the material world rather than the spiritual world. On the contrary, the material world is based on the concept of samsara that is a world of 'make believe' or 'illusion' because it gets destroyed with passage of time. Seekers believe that the material world is actually unreal and things as they seem on the outside are not what they really are! Seekers consider the spiritual world as '*Om Tat Sat*' and the cosmos as the absolute truth, implying that the spiritual realm is eternal in nature and hence is real. Thus, both worlds become real and unreal depending upon the perception of the soulprint. This duality leads to an imbalance in our lives as we try to live in one world at a time and loose focus of the other.

The wisdom of the Bhagavad Gita is multifold and its wisdom pertaining to the spiritual and material disconnect is discussed in this chapter. The Gita, which provides the complete spiritual science, in essence also describes the wisdom of the five sheaths. When your inner dots are connected in a systematic way, limitless energy flows from your soul dot to the intellect, emotive dot, and life breath and eventually powers your body dot into action. The Gita explains this connection in terms of yoga (meaning yuj or connection in Sanskrit) and propagates the four paths to spiritual providence.

The Four Paths of Yoga in the Gita

Dhyana Yoga or the science of meditation, describes the connection to the soul dot and was discussed in Chapter 3. To connect the body, emotive and intellect dots to the soul, the wisdom of Karma Yoga is relevant. Karma Yoga is the science of the interconnections of the inner dots with the soul dot and this was discussed in the previous chapter. Gyana Yoga describes the science of the intellectual dot and its relationship with the emotive dot and is discussed in this chapter. Bhakti Yoga or the behavioural science of faith and devotion, describes the connection of the soul dot with the Super Soul, which is discussed in the next chapter.

Mahabharata: A Soulful Story

The Gita, is a part of the epic Mahabharata, which describes not only social and human behaviour, but also delves into the inner conflicts of an individual. Such conflicts beget choices for individuals, who often make them without realizing the truth in them from their level of consciousness. A few people might choose to be self focused like King Dhrishrashtra who got blinded by the love of his sons while others might choose to be altruistic like Bhishama Pithama, who though was soulful and had renounced his throne and life for the greater good of the kingdom but still found himself on the wrong side of righteousness on the battlefield.

Every person in the epic has a deep inner story to share, which can help any seeker to realize part of the truth on his or her own spiritual journey. This epic has immense depth and scope that helps the seeker in gaining insights into multiple perspectives, as each character has its own reasons and beliefs in the choices they make. Thus, Mahabharata is considered to be a complete epic depicting all facets of the human behaviour. For a better understanding of how the intellect dot works, a small yet relevant, section of the Gita is discussed below from the perspective of the great warrior prince Arjuna.

Arjuna's Predicament

When Arjuna reached the battleground and saw the two warring sides of the Kuru dynasty (to which he belonged), he found himself faced with a tough decision as to whether he should fight with his loved ones or not. On seeing the stark duality of life, where someone was a loved family member, a guru or a friend in one instance and enemy in the other, Arjuna broke down in front of Lord Krishna, his charioteer, friend, philosopher and guide. Arjuna declared that he did not have any will, nor reason, to fight with his near and dear ones.

Arjuna's *predicament was of his intellect dot.* He used logic to justify his decision to not fight. Further in the epic, Arjuna said that his 'body quivered and his mouth dried up' at the mere thought of fighting with his near and dear ones. He also implied that he got no 'pleasure' from winning the battle, for living in luxury did not attract him. Arjuna's contention was that when his intelligence did not equate winning the battle with pleasure then why should he wage it! The other reason he gave was that the battle would lead to the collective destruction of the Kuru dynasty, which would further lead to loss of collective knowledge and wisdom, hence there was no logic to cause such a massive setback to the Kuru dynasty or the prevalent world order! Finally, he reasoned that since he was confused and conflicted, a state of mental chaos had engulfed him and he was unable to rely on his intellect to take the right decision. Thus, he thought that the best course for him was not to fight and *surrendered himself to Lord Krishna for guidance.*

Arjuna's arguments make complete sense when you look at them from an intellectual perspective. Even today, there are many instances where your intellect is unable to decide. '*To do or not to do?' has been a million-realization question for many of us.* You must often find yourself in a state of confusion and darkness. Sometimes you are not able to decide how to choose between your own good vis-à-vis the greater good. When the stakes are very high for the intellect to understand and decide, emotive and spiritual chaos follows and the whole body system falls apart. For instance, a person's decision to commit suicide stems from their mental confusion and resignation to the limited and undesirable choices before them, in that moment.

Lord Krishna's Solution

Lord Krishna addressed Arjuna's predicament from the perspective of Arjuna. This means that the decision you take should always be taken from *your perspective, that is, from your position, your soulprint and your context, and not of any one else.* Lord Krishna did not answer the question from his own perspective. He espoused that a decision for your self, no matter how noble, can be construed as immoral if taken by another soulprint instead of you. For instance, a doctor's perspective in treating a patient is different from the hospital owner's perspective, and a doctor might face a dilemma when he is filling the doctor's shoes in a hospital that is also owned by him! For a decision to be taken, one has to step into the shoes of the person who is taking the decision. In such an instance, if a medical decision has to be taken on the operating table then the decision maker should wear the 'doctor's hat'. However, if the decision is to be taken from an administrative point of view, then the decision maker must wear the owner's hat.

Lord Krishna told Arjuna that, being a warrior and a protector of the Kuru dynasty, he had to conform to a higher moral ground when taking decisions, as any decision he took would become the precedent for future leaders and societies. Hence, it was imperative that Arjuna took this decision, to fight the ideological war, as a leader of the Pandu family and custodian of righteousness, not as a brother or a friend or a well wisher of the family.

Lord Krishna further clarified that Arjuna's *compassion* was misplaced. Arjuna's compassion in essence was towards his own intellect, that is, 'his' kith and 'his' kin, which are in relation to his emotive dot identity. His compassion was not stemming from his soul dot, which envisioned greater good for everyone in the world order.

When you see the world from the perspective of your soul (soulful state), then you have a different realization of what you should or should not do, and what is right or wrong. Thus for Arjuna, fighting for the righteous in society has a bigger and a different purpose than fighting (or not fighting) for his own self-interests. Shri Krishna thus showed Arjuna the path of soulful living and advised him to not get caught in his emotive identity of 'my family' and 'my teachers' to solve his predicament. Arjuna had to lead by example by letting go of his self-interest and perhaps even give up his life for the greater good of the world. Your focus on your purpose of being in the current life and form supersedes all other purposes that might be created along the way. For instance, call to duty for the soldier guarding the Indian borders is the most respected and coveted life's calling, and Arjuna's call was no different. Hence, one's soul's perspective of answering life's purpose is superior to the affinity to one's kith and kin.

In the same way, you should look at your challenges from the perspective of your soul when taking decisions. Like Arjuna, you too will be driven only by your intellect at the beginning of your spiritual journey and how to deal with your intellect is a million-realization learning. Lord Krishna further provided three answers to pacify Arjuna's intellectual predicament. Satisfying intellectual debates are as important as addressing spiritual dilemmas, else you might take irrational decisions and confuse faith and blind faith. It is rationality that distinguishes a spiritual seeker from a mere follower of a religion.

Lord Krishna told Arjuna that he should not negate the importance of wealth and power that will accrue to him on winning the war. The natural rule of survival of the fittest should be followed and maintained. Shri Krishna reiterated that this was an ideological fight. So Arjuna must use his intellect to fight ignorance, as it would take him towards higher spiritual development. On victory, he would get all the material world wealth and glory, which could be used to spread righteousness in the world. However, if Arjuna does not fight then his stature as a leader would diminish, which is 'worse than death' for a person of his repute and position. Hence, Arjuna needed to value his intellectual prowess to fight. You too need to value, trust and *use* your intelligence when you have to take a critical decision. Doubting your intelligence is not the way forward!

Lord Krishna reassured Arjuna that there will be no obliteration of the Kuru dynasty if Arjuna engages in war with his relatives and loved ones because everyone on this planet has a lifespan and will die someday only to be reborn. Thus, the death of *his* kith and kin was irrelevant. However, what was relevant was the purpose of living. On Arjuna's victory, righteousness would prosper in current lifetime and also would be enjoyed by all souls taking rebirth on this planet in the future. So, Arjuna, in this life, had to perform his duties to spread 'light' and wisdom. Since this war had a higher purpose, it was necessary for Arjuna to fight it in order to maintain the righteous world order.

Understanding the concept of rebirth is one of the most important aspects of spiritual wisdom as without knowing the eternal nature of the soul, spiritual wisdom cannot be realized in entirety. Many religions do not believe in rebirth, and find it difficult to differentiate between the intellect and the soul, as they seem inseparable during a lifetime.

Rebirth is the cyclical process for evolution of the soul, which interconnects the spiritual world with the manifested world. In this concept, when a person dies and leaves the material world, his soulprint at a later time manifests back into a new life form and takes rebirth as a newborn child. When this soulprint is reborn, it gets a new body dot along with a new family, new place and hence it experiences a 'new' reality for itself. This cycle of rebirth forms the essence of spiritual science, which makes the soul eternal in its existence.

Further, this science explains that you choose your new body dot depending upon what you were seeking, at the time you departed in your previous lifetime. Thus, the true purpose of your current life is to enlighten your soulprint to higher realizations, as your next life will be based on your current realizations of spiritual wisdom. It also implies that one should enlighten or improve the material world, as it will be used by other soulprints on their rebirth. This 'new' reality is in fact an existing reality for the family in which the soulprint has taken rebirth. The forefathers of that family have now taken rebirth in a different place in this world and have inherited some other existing reality. When everyone works on this concept of truth, then everyone will get a better world on rebirth and then evolution of mankind will accelerate. Further, the science of rebirth postulates that the body is like a rented house for a soul and you should not get attached to your life's successes or failures. Hence, one needs to make his acts soulful without attaching one's desires to them.

Lord Krishna reiterated that all acts, including the ideological war, leading to destruction of ignorance are justified for Arjuna as such non-selfish acts are required to maintain the soulful world order.

Lord Krishna finally concluded that Arjuna's confusion in taking the decision was misplaced because Arjuna considered himself to be the doer, hence the enjoyer or beneficiary of his actions. He had to see it from the perspective of his soul; he had to realize that his body was only participating on behalf of the eternal self, which in fact is part of the Super Soul. He needed to take decisions not only for his own awakening but also for the awakening of the world order.

The Essence of Gyana Yoga

Your soulprint has a unique perspective that is relevant only to you and your existence, and you can realize it only by awakening it. The sooner you balance your outer world with the relevance of your inner world, the faster you will progress towards your awakening. When the will to fight a battle comes from the soul's (Arjuna's) perspective, that is, of greater good, then it is justified as opposed to when it comes from fulfilling the selfish desires of the ego (Duryodhana's, the other side's perspective). Thus, to make sense of your actions you need to see the context of the five inner dots in your everyday living—soulful vs. intellectual vs. emotive vs. physical. The deeper you think, the higher the path unfolds. This wisdom of the Gyana Yoga is relevant to awaken your soulprint and the way forward for soulful living.

7

LOVE THY NEIGHBOUR

In your journey so far, you have discovered the inner dots, understood their nature and delved deeper into understanding the intellect relationship with the soulful self. However, the journey would be futile if you do not explore the wisdom of the emotive self and the ways to connect it to the Super Soul. Many people give more power to emotions and believe that it fosters stronger bonds than intellectual ones as it chooses to attach rather than work on the wisdom to detach as experienced through other yogas. Your desires drive you to realize outrageous possibilities even when they seem irrational as your likes and dislikes cannot always be logically explained. For instance, for parents it is not an intellectual decision to have children but an emotional one. All pure desires and wishes are not based out of the intellect. However, once the emotive self bubbles with desires, the intellect works towards making them a reality by contemplating ways to accomplish them. A wish, in this way, becomes an actionable thought and gets converted into actions and you experience the new reality based on such aspirations.

Emotive vs. Soulful Desires

When you make your emotive dot the master of your actions, then you focus to *self-please* yourself. The emotive self becomes both the doer and enjoyer of the actions. Your brain not only thinks what is pleasurable, but also releases happy hormones when your body does such acts in the self-pleasure maximization mode. In this mode, you only choose to gratify your senses with things that give you a 'kick'. For instance, when you buy a luxury car, the admiration of people around you gives your ego a kick and you end up buying more things of similar nature to show off, irrespective of whether you want them. Pursuing such pleasures might give you the false impression that you are living a fulfilling life. When the emotive and intellect dots become self-focused, then you exist in an egoistical state. This existence is no different from that of a drug addict who gets high on consuming drugs! In this state, you do not feel that you need anyone and do not even see the need to be soulful to feel the 'kick' or the energy boost. This ignorance leads to a state of self-glorification, which is like an inflated balloon filled with gas rather than a cloud of consciousness filled with realizations. This imbalance between your self-focused dots (ego) and your soul dot causes a spiritual gap within you. In this state, you feel pleasurable but not happy. For example, you could consume your favourite food but may not get any satisfaction. You might have multiple partners but feel no joy when you spend time with any one of them. In such a state, you will be constantly seeking the next thing for experiencing happiness. Happiness is not experienced by fulfilling your desires but by realizing that you are already in a state of abundance.

When you act from the perspective of your soul then you attain a state of perfect happiness, and when you act from any other lower level perspective then you experience pleasure. For instance, when you eat a meal as an offering to the Super Soul (prashad), then your focus shifts from pleasure maximization towards compassion and gratitude for the cosmos. On the other hand, when you eat from the perspective of self-consumption then you only focus on maximizing your own pleasures and your stomach becomes a bottomless pit. The state of happiness cannot coexist with greediness. For this reason, all religions encourage offering a prayer to the Almighty before eating any meal. Many religions also encourage followers to think of the Universe first by offering their first serving of a meal (say) to a cow, as practised in Hinduism, or giving alms to the needy while visiting the place of worship, as practised in Islam.

The Million-Realization Question

A Million-Realization Question is what truly makes a wish moral (good) or immoral (bad) one? The emotive dot is where all your desires germinate. Your intellect contemplates and works to realize your desires. However, the wish that comes from a soulful (moralistic) state, gets the wind of the ecosystem behind it as they are aligned with it whereas the wish that comes from the self focused emotive state gets pulled down by the weight of its own ignorance and ego. In essence, when you connect your emotive dot with your soul and make the soul its master, you aspire to a higher place filled with goodness and garner all-round support towards the fulfilment of your wish. Thus, your moralistic desires make the world a better place and take your complete life experience to a higher state.

Yoga: the Path to Connect the Super Soul

There are four tools of soulful living that increase your spiritual metabolism for soulful living namely—spiritual wisdom (Gyana Yoga), spiritual practice (Krama Yoga), faith (Dhyana Yoga) and devotion (Bhakti Yoga). All the four paths of yoga, namely, Karma,

Bhakti, Gyana and Dhyana, are different in their wisdom, orientation and practice. You are present at different levels of consciousness at different times in your life and so all these paths of yoga need to be jointly pursued. No one path alone can help you connect with the Super Soul. Proper connection of your inner dots provides limitless nutrition for the growth of your soulprint just as an umbilical cord connects and feeds a foetus in the womb. The connection to the Super Soul as explained by Bhakti Yoga is unique as it works on the philosophy of attachment, contrary to other yogas, which advocate detachment.

Bhakti Yoga

Bhakti Yoga is the devotional connect with the higher power when your emotive dot takes the lead. Out of all the different paths of yoga like Dhyana Yoga, Karma Yoga and Gyana Yoga, Bhakti or the emotive connect, has become the mainstay of all religions. This includes bhajans or devotional songs in Hinduism, gospels and sermons in Christianity, Sufism in Islam and singing in the synagogues in Judaism. 'Bhakti' means devotion and it connects a soulprint in the feeling of love and surrender to the Super Soul.

Types of Bhakti

As per the Indic literature there is 'saguni' bhakti or form (idol) worship and the 'nirguni' bhakti or formless worship of the Super Soul. Epics like the Ramayana and Mahabharata deal with saguni bhakti with Lord Vishnu as the Super Soul who incarnates as Lord Ram and Lord Krishna. On the other hand, Jainism, Buddhism, Sikhism, and poets like Kabir, Rumi champion the nirguni bhakti aspect of spirituality where there are absence of any human form to offer prayers. Irrespective of the school of bhakti, Bhakti Yoga is integral spiritual science of connect and no connection to the Super Soul can ever be complete without the devotion of a soulprint.

Emotions are integral to human psychology. When you connect with your parents, then such a connect is not based on logic and is not transactional in nature. The left side of the brain performs tasks that have to do with logic, such as in science and mathematics. The right side of the brain performs tasks that have to do with creativity and the arts. Spiritual wisdom covers both the emotive science of human behaviour as well as the intellectual (or rational) principles. Undeniably, when you exude affection and love then the energy or vibrations are infectious and are felt all around you. The spiritual connect should always be about your personal conversations with the Super Soul and only your soulful intentions should be the focus of all your actions. However, the only caveat to this kind of emotion-based connection to the Super Soul is that you should not get blown away with emotional irrationality. Also, your actions should be done with focus on inner soul dot rather than on impressing others.

The Bhavas

As a matter of fact, the Vedic discourse puts more weight on the 'bhava' or 'bhavana', meaning pure intentions rather than the resultant action. The same idea is revered in Jainism, Buddhism, Christianity and even Islam. In Hinduism, there are many folk stories about ascertaining one's intentions as the deciding force of what is correct or not. One of the most interesting Krishna Bhakti stories in this regard, goes as follows.

Once a wealthy merchant decided to value Lord Krishna in the weight of gold coins for donation to the needy. When Lord Krishna sat on the weighing scale, the merchant, to his surprise, was unable to tilt the weighing balance on his side with abundant gold coins. He soon realized his mistake and gave up his ego and in complete devotion placed the leaves of a Tulsi plant (considered to be auspicious in a Hindu household) on the weight scale, which finally tilted in the merchant's favour because this act depicted his complete surrender to Lord Krishna, the Super Soul. Measuring one's devotion is an impossible task and only one's 'bhav' or piety of intentions can encapsulate its magnitude.

Thus, bhava is bigger than material wealth or actions and this is an accepted belief across religions. Ibrahim's willingness to sacrifice his son on God's order is one such example. In Judaism, 'bhava' is given utmost importance and referred to as 'kavanah'. Our intentions are more important than the results of our actions. *In the material world we focus on the outcomes of one's actions whereas the spiritual world, we focus on the intentions.*

The Science of Faith

A Million-Realization Question is how do we emotionally connect with the Super Soul when it is not present on earth? Is idol-worship the right way to connect with the Super Soul? Is there any science behind any religious practices or are all of them completely irrational?

The science behind faith and devotion is proven by the 'Placebo effect'. When you believe something to be true then the Universe and your body dot make it true. Many patients have known to be cured of ailments on non-medicinal pills just because they believed it to be the cure. Similarly, faith works on the principle of belief. When you believe the stone sculpture in a temple to be the human manifestation of the Super Soul or God then the idol can work wonders and connect you to the Super Soul. However, when a corrupt clergy tries to con you, then you need to believe with your eyes open, not shut.

Secondly, everyone has a soul, which is in essence a part of the creator. Hence, when you connect with other soulprints who are part of the Super Soul, you, in essence, spiritually connect to the Super Soul. Taking care of God's children, the fellow souls, is therefore critical to soulful living. How can you shun your fellow souls and keep peace with the Super Soul? Charity beings at home and so does your connect with the Universe. Hinduism has described this human connect in terms of five bhavanas or emotive connects, in general with the Super Soul and specifically with the people.

1. Parental love or Vatsalya Bhava
2. Brotherhood love or Shakhya Bhava
3. Devotional love or Dasya Bhava
4. Peaceful love or Shanta Bhava
5. Consort love or Madhurya Bhava

As you connect with others through various relationships, you must be soulful and foster compassion and love for others. To love thy neighbour is the easiest way to connect with the Super Soul, as all souls in essence are part of the Super Soul. In Krishna Bhakti literature, all emotive bhavas are showered on Shri Krishna, an avatar of the Super Soul Lord Vishnu, who has been praised through many such wonderful stories about his various incarnations or swarups on earth over periods of time.

For Instance, parental love has been depicted in tales of Krishna and his mother Yashoda; brotherhood love is visible in the stories of Balarama and Sudama; devotional love resonates in the songs of Meerabai; peaceful love overflows in the narratives on the people of Braj (Lord Krishna's hometown) and consort love is encapsulated in the Lord Krishna leelas or divine play with Radha.

Navratna Malika or the Nine Spiritual Acts

The practice of emotive connect is described in the Bhagvad Purana, a revered text in Vaishnavism, which is part of Hindu tradition that reveres Lord Vishnu. The emotive connect to the Super Soul can be inculcated in daily life by the practice of any or all of the 'Navratna Malika' or nine spiritual acts:

1. *Sravana* or listening to the glories or activities of the Super Soul
2. *Kirtan* or chanting the words of wisdom of the Super Soul
3. S*imrana* or remembering the glories of the Super Soul
4. *Padaseva* or feeling of service (seva) for the Super Soul
5. *Archana* or worshipping the Super Soul
6. *Namaskar/ Vandana* or feeling of respect for the Super Soul
7. *Dasya* or feeling of servitude to the Super Soul
8. *Sakhyatva* or feeling of friendship towards the Super Soul
9. *Atma Nivedan* or feeling of complete surrender to the Super Soul

Practice of these nine spiritual acts does not necessarily mean that you have to sing or dance or play music on loudspeakers to keep everyone awake all through the night in order to please and connect with the Super Soul. On the contrary, hurting any other soul through any act is a regressive step in one's spiritual path. Inculcate these acts of devotion peacefully in your everyday life. If you truly believe that the cosmos is the manifestation of the Super Soul and the human race is part of the cosmos, then activities such as serving food or water to the needy, respecting elderly people at home or work, loving your neighbour, treating everyone as a friend and not foe, taking care of the underprivileged or disadvantageous groups, should be considered as devotional love to other souls and in essence towards the Super Soul. In this way, you connect your emotive self to the Super Soul and feel energized and calm from within. Thus by placing the Super Soul at a higher level to your own soul and thereby making it a master of your soul, which in turn is the master of all your inner dots, the flow of energy is clearly defined, and this unison 'maketh of a realized soul'.

SECTION 2

EMBODIMENT—CONNECT TO THE UNIVERSE

8

EVOLUTION OF SPIRITUAL WISDOM

In the first part of your spiritual journey, you connected to your inner cosmos to achieve a higher state of self-realization. The second phase of the spiritual development is to connect with the higher power. Without the connection to the collective spiritual wisdom present all around you, your existence is not only incomplete, but also limited in purpose. Before striving to establish your personal connection, first understand, that how individuals and communities throughout history have tried to connect with the higher power or the Super Soul. It does help to seek wisdom from the past to make the future brighter. In the past, such connects of the individuals and the communities have given birth to religions of the world. Many such religions have faded away and many have prospered. As the existence of a religious practice does not make it right or a relevant one, similarly fading away of a spiritual thought does not make it irrelevant. You need to be unbiased and exploratory when understanding any religion or spiritual practice in the context of time and place of human evolution to learn from it for your journey ahead!

Spirituality vs. Religion

When all religions connect to the Super Soul for peace and happiness, then why is there non-alignment among them? Why is interaction of one religion with another a contentious issue?

> *What is made, cannot maketh, what is unmade.*
>
> Chandogya Upanishad

This means, what is made (religion), cannot maketh (make), what is unmade (spirituality), that is, religion cannot make spirituality. Once humanity makes spirituality or a spiritual thought, apt in a certain context and practised into a 'religious movement', then that religious movement finds it impossible to go back into the spiritual realm and further evolve that spiritual thought for betterment of all the soulprints. Just like milk once converted into curd, cannot be converted back into milk, comparably religion once formed cannot go back to the spiritual wisdom it had germinated from in the first place. In spiritual realm, all paths (religious and social) are equal and relevant and each soulprint needs to choose for itself. For instance, the concept to 'convert' a person to 'my religion', does not have any basis in the spiritual realm. For two souls, to commit to a relationship, like a marriage, should not be a matter of religious beliefs but spiritual ones. Hence, on enforcing such religious conversions spirituality is lost and religious ignorance perpetuates. The essence of every religion should be traced back to its spiritual wisdom, and when we seek that wisdom in any religion's practices, we in essence seek the spirit of its true purpose.

East vs. West

The spiritual world can be divided into two sides—the East and the West. The eastern and the western regions were on the two sides of the ancient river Indus. It is difficult to ascertain the terrain and the civilizations that might have existed at that time which demarcated the two sides, however, that distinction is clear from the current reflection on history of spirituality and its evolution. The Indus Valley Civilization (named after the Indus River) was a Bronze Age Civilization in the north-western regions of South Asia, lasting from 3300 BCE to 1300 BCE, and in its mature form from 2600 BCE to 1900 BCE. Many things are unknown about this civilization, but what is commonly known is that spiritual DNA of the western region was distinct from that of the eastern side to the Indus, that is, the region of the Indian subcontinent. Interestingly, reminisced evolution of spirituality started somewhere between 2000 BCE and 1000 BCE in both the regions.

The western region saw the rise of Abrahamic religions based on the lives of Abraham and Sarah, believed to have existed around 1700 BCE. The first religion propagated in this region was Judaism, which later gave birth to Christianity around 1st century CE, and eventually to Islam around 600 CE. Judaism and Christianity developed into many regionalized variants of evolved beliefs and practises whereas Islam split into two prominent sects—the Sunni and the Shia.

On the other hand, spiritualism in the eastern region, that is, the Indian subcontinent was practised as 'a way of life'. The wisdom on life and living in its cultural and social aspects and its alignment with the cosmos was called 'Sanatan Dharma', and geographically referred to as Hinduism. The word 'sanatan' means 'eternal', and 'dharma' means the 'natural flow of truth', that is, 'the human's duty as per the eternal laws of nature'. This eternal knowledge encapsulated by the experiences and realizations of its practioners led to evolution of knowledge called the Vedas. The Vedas and the Upanishads are believed to have originated during the period 1000-2000 BCE (or earlier) and evolved through many oral and written deliberations of the practitioners of Sanatan Dharma. For people in this region, religion meant a way of life that described and prescribed one's social and moral duties. A person born into this belief system or who choose to follow the basic principles of Sanatan Dharma is called a Hindu. The word 'Hindu' comes from the word 'Sindhu', the local name for the river Indus. It came into being as the Persians pronounced 'Sindhu' as 'Hindu'. Thus, Sanatan Dharma encapsulates the set of ethical duties and ordained practices incumbent upon all *Hindus* for their everyday life as deemed necessary, both individually and collectively.

Spiritualism In The East–The Indian Subcontinent

The south-eastern region of the Indus practised dharmic philosophy as a way of life, just like Taoism that is also based on the eternal law of nature. However, the majority of the population of the Indian subcontinent, was and still is, consists of the 'religiously unclassified' section called the believers of Hinduism. Hinduism's way of life formed the genesis of other prominent religions in this region such as Jainism, Buddhism, Sikhism.

Hinduism

Unlike the modern schooling system, the Vedic education was based on the teachings of the spiritual realm and the cosmos. The same was encapsulated in the Vedas and the Upanishads. Initially, spirituality pervaded all parts of everyday living based on the assumption that what is 'inside' (soulful) of a person is on the 'outside', that is, people did what they said, and said what they thought and thought what they believed. So, in this ancient age of soulful living, all decisions, choices and actions were based from the perspective of the Soul. Everyone abided by the same set of said and unsaid principles. These principles became the rules for governing an individual's conduct vis-à-vis their life's activities as well as their social interactions with the other people in their community. Thus, Hinduism referred to the culture and beliefs of the people living in the region, without any holy book or a prophet. Since no one can trace its origins, it is revered as 'a way of life that always existed', hence called Sanatan. Sanatan Dharma inculcates a life based on the Eternal Law, that is, the law that *always existed, still exists and will always exist–the natural way!*

The Vedas and Upanishads

The philosophy and teachings of Hinduism were captured primarily in the Vedas and the Upanishads, which evolved over thousands of years and were initially transmitted orally through generations. The word 'Veda' comes from the root word 'vid' or 'vidya' meaning 'knowledge' colloquially referred to as 'the encyclopaedia of Spiritual Wisdom. And the word 'Upanishad' is a conjugation of three words 'Upa-ni-shad' meaning 'close-low-sit' denoting the style of teaching in the guru-shishya tradition with the student sitting at a lower level (in humility) to his guru. The Vedas, in essence, were about an individual's journey and the Upanishads were about guiding others on their journey, and both were based on empirically verifiable knowledge, interactions and teachings. For instance, Ayurveda comes from the world 'Ayush' meaning 'life', and Veda meaning knowledge, that is, 'the knowledge for a healthy life'. It is a 5,000-year-old system of natural healing as practiced in the Vedic period. The medical practitioners or doctors of the time delved into the healing properties of various plants and substances and prescribed health solutions. For instance, keeping a Tulsi plant at home is one such practice, as the plant has many medicinal properties and hence is a positive source of maintaining a healthy life.

In many stories of the Upanishads, the gurus came up with

creative ways of teaching for their shishyas (students) to realize the truth instead of just telling them of the facts; this encouraged the students to seek and realize the truth themselves which is the whole purpose of any education system. Fundamentally, the four Vedas in Hinduism, are steeped in wisdom, are actually the four sciences to understand the environment or the cosmos.

- The Rig Veda (the knowledge of songs and mantras of praises for the cosmos, that is the soul dot)
- Yajur Veda (the knowledge of how to perform rituals for worship, that is the intellect dot)
- Sama Veda (the knowledge of melodies and arts, that is the emotive dot)
- the Atharva Veda also called Ayur Veda (the knowledge of life in the physical form, that is the body dot).

Therefore, all the 'teachings' were sorted into categories corresponding to the four bodies/sheaths (spiritual, intellectual, emotional and physical body) thereby encapsulating the timeless wisdom of how the natural forces and elements in the cosmos interact with the complete human self.

The 'Custodians'

It was wrongfully propagated that the wisdom of the Vedas and the Upanishads as encapsulated in the Ramayana, Mahabharata and Bhagavad Purana was privy to only the priesthood or Brahmin community, who were the custodians of this wisdom and later became the sole 'owners' of this knowledge. People who were entrusted with the responsibility of managing and transferring the wisdom of Brahman (the Cosmos) to the future generations were called 'Brahmans' in Sanskrit, or 'Brahmins' in English language. Initially being a 'Brahmin' was a matter of one's life choice, but soon it became a hereditary practice. Priests started to 'own' the spiritual wisdom as their birthright. They imparted Vedic knowledge only to their kith and kin and forbade non-Brahmins to even listen to its words thereby creating a divide in the society. For instance, stories in the epic Mahabharata like that of the under privileged Eklavya are case in point to this malpractice. This led to a trust deficit between the 'custodians' of the spiritual power and the masses. Further, misinterpretations of the texts by the custodians for personal gain, lead to massive exploitation of the masses who found themselves culturally bound with the dharmic laws on ways of living without even knowing the essence of those religious and social practices. For instance, a poor man's son was forced to spend excessively on the last rites of his deceased father by the custodians with a promise to make his father's next lifetime comfortable thereby further impoverishing the son's current life! Religion became a way to extract money from the believers in the form of expensive ritualistic practices, like Ashvamedha (or the horse sacrifice), havans or community feasts and forced donations to temples. This resulted in a lack of proper understanding of spirituality and created an ardent need for an alternate practice. This was realized in the form of the Jain philosophy of living.

Jainism

Jainism comes from the word 'jina', which means the conqueror. In this context, a conqueror is a person who has *won over his inner desires and longings*. According to Jainism, there were twenty-four Tirthankars or enlightened souls with 'Adi Nath' being the first one and Mahavira being the last one. Mahavira is said to have lived around sixth century BCE. 'Adi' means the first, and 'Nath' means 'the Lord', that is *the first enlightened one*, whereas 'Mahavira' comes from the conjugation of two words, 'maha' meaning 'the great' and 'vira' meaning the 'warrior', implying *the person who conquered his inner self like no one else*. Jainism propagated five unique moralistic rules, which differentiated it from the general malpractices of the Hindu clergy at the time. These rules were

- non-violence,
- truthfulness,
- non-stealing,
- celibacy and
- non-accumulation of wealth.

Interestingly, the Brahmins for their selfish reasons had in essence wrongly practiced these five virtues. Jainism, like the earlier practice, continued with the role of the clergy in one's spiritual development but with a strict adherence to these five virtues. Jain philosophy clearly distinguished two paths—one for the clergy and the other for its followers. Followers were respected and considered beginners in their spiritual journey. The clerics of Jainism practiced what they preached and emphasized worship based on inner reflections rather than outer ritualistic practice, as prescribed by the Brahmins of the time. For example, the Jains completely rejected the sacrificial killing of animals, which was common in the Vedic times. In essence, the clergy led the path of spiritual evolution whereas the Jain followers (as seekers) observed and inculcated clergy's values in the best way they could in their everyday living.

In Jainism, the clergy was divided into two schools of thought the Digambara and the Svetambara. The Digambaras, or the 'sky clad' (implying without any clothes on their body), believed in the cosmos protecting and encompassing all its beings and hence philosophically they did not feel the need for even wearing clothes. The Svetambaras, or the 'white clad', held the same beliefs but chose to travel and reach out to the householders in spreading their spiritual wisdom and chose to adorn clothing in white colour only. It is interesting to see that the essence of Vedic wisdom, where humans tried to align themselves with the cosmos, was the basis of practices of Jainism.

Out of many beliefs, the central philosophy in Jainism was of 'anekanta-vada', which means 'many perspectives or opinions', that is, acceptance of multiple facets of the truth, which was contrary to the Brahmin's way of practice. This meant more power was given to the different perspectives of reality as experienced by the seekers. Jainism emphasized ideal worship over idol worship. The lifestyle of the Jain clergy depicted the philosophy of inner and outer asceticism, that is, renunciation of the desires as well as of the material wealth. This became a visual example for the followers to learn that a soulful life is possible even without chasing material wealth. However, under Jainism the only path available for spiritual awakening to a true seeker was one of extreme asceticism. Further, it did not offer any solutions for personal spiritual advancement for the family men or the house dwellers. Seekers were left with a difficult option to either follow the exploitative Brahmin practices or to become clerics themselves and negate their attachments altogether for their spiritual pursuits. This growing gap between the two extremist ways of life was bridged by Buddhism.

Buddhism

Gautama Buddha was the founder of Buddhism around 563 BCE–483 BCE. The word 'Buddha' comes from the Sanskrit word 'buddhi' meaning 'the wisdom' and hence the word means the 'awakened one'. Buddha and Mahavira are believed to be contemporaries. Both believed in the individualistic approach to seeking the truth.

Buddha emphasised on individual spiritual experience, instead of reliance on priests. This negation of the role of the clergy empowered the seeker to carry on their spiritual journey themselves. Mahavira, belonging to a modest household, was introduced to ascetic rules of Jainism very early in his life. In contrast, Prince

Siddartha (Buddha's real name) lived a life of opulence for the first eighteen odd years of his life. Soon after his son was born, Prince Siddartha left his home and hearth in quest for the truth. Buddha's journey on the spiritual path started with the practice of extreme asceticism, perhaps based on Jain principles prevalent at the time. His initial followers were in fact Jain monks who were seeking wisdom in the jungle at that time. As Buddha wandered in the jungles of Uruvela (central India) to seek inner awakening, he gave up food and water for days and did not wear any protective clothing. After close encounters with death, Buddha realized that extreme asceticism is not the way ahead for a seeker. Hence, after enlightenment Buddha shared the wisdom of the 'middle path' with all the seekers. The middle path propagated a normal living for the householder along with the spiritual practice of non-violence, non-attachment, non-stealing and non-lying. He collapsed the need for the clergy and encouraged the seeker to be responsible for his own journey. Buddha, in contrast to Mahavira, was more exploratory and experimental as he chose to leave behind what his parents asked him to follow and created a revolutionary movement based on new spiritual wisdom, whereas Mahavira strictly accepted his parents belief system and ardently followed the existing Jainism tenets. The middle path and the exploratory nature of Buddha proved to be a boon for people who were neither willing nor able to follow the existing paths of Brahamic domination or Jain asceticism.

The most popular follower of Buddhism was the king Ashoka, the great emperor of the Maurya dynasty, who accepted Buddha's teachings somewhere in the year 268 BCE. Ashoka, who enjoyed abundance of wealth and power, realized that material wealth was no substitute for inner peace and happiness. In this realization, Ashoka ensured that the preachings of Buddhism were spread both in India and abroad, especially Southeast Asia. Buddhism advocated a balanced approach in one's life for attaining nirvana and Buddhist philosophy made a huge course correction in the evolution of spiritual wisdom across the world.

However, spread of Buddhism had its own set of challenges. The first challenge was both linguistic and cultural. The language used in the initial Buddhist discourse was Pali, in place of Sanskrit. Sanskrit was and still is intertwined with Vedic philosophy to the extent that it's impossible to separate the two fully. Jainism was propagated in Prakrit, which was akin to Sanskrit. Thus the key religious custodians of the time (Jain and Hindu) were not open to 'foreign invasion' of the new Buddhist thoughts and language. One other challenge towards acceptance came from the philosophy of the 'middle path' that works when a person has a choice between a life of opulence and a life of asceticism, like a king or a rich person. However, the masses at the time were struggling in their day-to-day activities and found themselves walking on the only path available to them, of putting bread on the table while staying away from any religious practices altogether. Ironically, at some level, many of us are still struggling with this life choice and have chosen to stay away from religious practices. Moreover, Buddhism's belief that the soul does not take rebirth negated the wisdom of the Upanishads as well as the wisdom of the Mahabharata and Ramayana and thus further muted its spread in the region. These factors and few others, led to easier spread of Buddhism more outside the Indian sub continent where Sanskrit was not used and Vedic wisdom had not been propagated before. It was not until the 6th century CE that a revolutionary thinking was brought forward by Shri Adi Shankaracharya, which led to the revival and reconstruction of Hinduism, as we know today.

Adi Shankracharya and the Revival of Hinduism

Shri Adi Shankracharya was born around 6th (or 8th as per conflicting records) century CE into a humble Hindu household in the Indian state of Kerala, to brahmin parents. From an early age, he understood the Vedas in immense detail. He propagated that the body and spirit are in fact one and every soul has to walk on its own path, which formed the basis of *Advait Vedanta philosophy*. He liberated Hinduism from the domination of Brahmins while connecting many temples, specially the four dhams present in 4 corners of Indian subcontinent, and empowering them as the spiritual headquarters. This helped to standardize the varied belief systems in different regions into one common philosophy. Through this consolidation of faith and decentralization of regional practices among the masses by Adi Shankracharya, Hinduism got the much required life force that was missing. He also explained the key differences between Buddhism and Hinduism; shortlisted 10 Upanishads as 'principal upanishads' out of the hundreds that were propagated. Further, he focused on the essence of the Vedas and gave more credence to thoughtfulness over action in one's spiritual development. Adi Shankaracharya's biggest contribution was to popularise Sanatan Dharma in its true form without making a religion out of it perhaps under his own name. The genesis of soulful living is based on the essence of this forgotten philosophy.

Sikhism

Sikhism comes from the word 'Sikh' (pronounced seekh), meaning a 'disciple' or a seeker. Sikhism is based on the teachings of Shri Guru Nanak (1469-1539 CE) and is articulated in the sacred scripture of Guru Granth Sahib. Sikhism is an offshoot of Hinduism through which mainstream Hinduism weathered the western disturbances, that is, Islam. The western spirituality came in the form of Islam, when the Mughal emperor Babar with an expansionist view invaded the eastern region of the Indus River in the 14th century CE. With this confluence, the religious conversion to Islam of the eastern population began. This is ironical because Islam itself was formed due to the expansionist nature of the Roman Empire. Around 16th century CE, the situation deteriorated to a level wherein two Sikh leaders namely Guru Arjan (1563 -1605) and Guru Tegh Bahadur (1621-1675) refused to convert to Islam and both were beheaded by the Mughal emperors. It was at this time that the centuries old Western spirituality, in the form of Islam, went to war with the centuries old Eastern spirituality, based on their fundamentally different ideologies and orientations. For the first time, the Eastern religions had to fight in the name of religion.

As Islam tried to install (conversion) the software of their spirituality by force, Hinduism with Sikhism at its forefront fought the battle. Sikhism advocated five 'Ks', namely kesh (uncut hair), khara (steel bracelet), kanga (a wooden comb), kaccha (underwear) and kirpan (steel sword) to be present with a true warrior (Sikh) at all times. The ideological battle was settled with the Mughal ruler's realization that the eastern side was willing to fight and die but not willing to convert from their way of living. To this effect, Sikhism was mostly adopted by the existing families in northern India of that time, in the states of Punjab alongside the Indus River. This limited the pace of invasion of Islam into the subcontinent, but did not stop it.

Sikhism brought all the different spiritual followers of the region under one banner to fight, as there were many regional sub-sects in Hinduism. Sikhism under Guru Nanak's wisdom, followed formless worship along with the acceptance of moral violence for self-defence. Till this time, Hinduism, Jainism and Buddhism propagated non-violence as their basic principle. However, Sikhism introduced the radical thought of moral violence, meaning, one can and must fight on moral grounds to solely protect one's spiritual existence. *Not every war is bad and not every peace is good.* The right to choose one's religion seemed to be an inherent right in the eastern region up to this point. With the advent of spiritual imperialism, people realized that spiritual democracy is a matter of soulprint's responsibility to fight for its spiritual freedom and cannot be taken for granted. Like a firewall in a computer, Sikhism protected and created a new way in the eastern region, which permitted co-existence of eastern spirituality with the western. As a result, Islam, Sanatan Dharma, Jainism, Buddhism and Sikhism have co-existed in equanimity in the sub-continent for centuries.

Christianity and the Indian Subcontinent

Christianity first came to the sub-continent in the 1st century CE. At the time, the linguistic and cultural differences between the apostles of the Church and the people of the coastal regions of the Indian subcontinent were an unsurmountable hurdle. The stories of Jesus Christ and the Jews were not resonating with the Eastern population who were unaware of European history. The number of people travelling on boats were also limited and hence Christianity was very limited in its spread at the time.

The second time Christianity came to the subcontinent was in the 16th century CE, with the expansion of the British Empire, when affordable water transportation became the centre of trade and commerce. Due to the Industrial Revolution, the focus of the British was purely industrial and commercial than religious. Moreover, the dominance of the Mughal dynasty in the subcontinent restricted the expansion of Christianity in the region. Hence, what could have become religious imperialism remained a financial domination and hence Christianity even in its second attempt wasn't adopted as much in the Indian subcontinent.

Western Spiritualism

Religions were formed based on ardent need of various regions of the world at the time. Religions initially stem from new insights that fill the gap between the spiritual wisdom and the material world practices. Thus when a new religion gets formed, it represents the ethical, political and social thoughts of the society relevant to that time and place. The new religious order brings wisdom to the people so they can be happy as well as successful at the same time. This is true not only for the Eastern spiritual history but also the Western. Organized spirituality or religion in the West began with Judaism.

Judaism

Judaism is believed to have existed since 1700 BCE. It starts with the lifetime of Abraham and Sarah based on the Abrahamic Covenant, which was a contractual commitment between God and Abraham. Judaism is called a 'covenant faith' as it is based on various covenants over a period of time, like the covenant made by Adam to not eat the apple from the tree in the garden of Eden, followed by many covenants made by Noah, Abraham, Jacob, Moses and others with the Super Soul. As per its historic beliefs, whenever people broke the covenant or its rules, they faced the wrath of God and thus were forced to correct their course. Judaism became prominent in the lives of people, with the lifetime of Moses, somewhere around 1200-1300 BCE.

The story unfolds with the King of Egypt, believed to be King Ramses, whose material wealth was exuberant, but his spiritual wisdom was almost non-existent. Symbolically, in the material world the masses were poor whereas in the spiritual world the pharaoh (the King) was the poorest. This was depicted in all the decisions he took for the masses of his kingdom. This led to an unrest that was brewing between the ruler and the ruled. For brevity, a battle was fought between the two sides, and with the help of divine intervention, a group of people led by Moses got victory and they envisioned a promised land, the country of Israel, as their final abode away from Egypt. The people of Israel formed the Jewish community at the time and were revered as the true believers of the new faith. Judaism was the first Western belief system that came up with the idea of a single, omnipresent, omniscient God (Yahweh) in place of many 'smaller' natural powers or cosmic Gods. The divine interventions implied special status of the Jews that further resulted in the belief system that Jews are 'the chosen' people of God and the rightful custodians of the spiritual wisdom. They ensured that even the words of their book were not shared with the people who are not 'worthy' of God's revelations. This alienated the non-Jews who were in fact a major part of the population present in and around those regions. This tension, between the Jews and the majority population, created unrest around 1st century CE, between the two sections, which paved way for Christianity, with the key underlining philosophy that all men are equal in the eyes of God.

Christianity

Christianity got wide acceptance in the 1st and 2nd century CE—after the birth of Jesus of Nazareth. As per the Christian beliefs, Christianity began with the crucifixion of Jesus Christ and his resurrection. Jesus Christ was a well learned Jew and due to his benevolent acts of sharing wisdom was looked upon as a teacher and revered as 'People's King' or 'King of the Masses'. Other Jewish leaders in that region, owing to their personal vendetta against Jesus Christ, deceitfully pitched Jesus Christ against the General of the provinces of the Roman Empire. Jesus Christ wanted to change a few of the 'unfair' Judaist practices of the time towards the non-Jews. Judaism forbade sharing of the revelations of God (in essence the spiritual wisdom) with the non-Jews, which Jesus of Nazareth disliked and protested against. Jesus Christ reached out to the 'not chosen' people in order to help them, to further their development both spiritually and intellectually. The spiritual ignorance of the

Roman administration could not answer the evolutionary need of the masses (non-Jews) thereby creating a spiritual gap, which was filled by Jesus Christ. With the sacrifice (crucifixion) of Jesus Christ, the non-Jews rose against the Roman administration. With the subsequent unrest of the masses, a new equilibrium was attained and Christianity was accepted by the Roman administration as a new soulful path.

The Christian leaders of that time were seekers and came up with the new thoughts partly based on the Jewish Hebrew Bible, and called their new holy book The New Testament. Christianity attracted all the new age scientists, scholars, architects, philosophers, artists and radical thinkers of the time, to charter a new course for the future. This is evident in the fact that they were able to change the time-keeping system from lunar to a solar system! The beautiful tall edifices and churches built, along with marvellous art and sculptures of the time are its testimonials. Christianity bridged the material and spiritual gap by giving power to the Church to influence the king's decision affecting the well being of the masses and in this way connected the collective spiritual wisdom of the empire with its leaders. With the expansion of the Roman Empire, Christian followers increased. This popularity became contentious as the Roman Empire, in its expansionist and imperialist mode, started dictating their systems and beliefs on their new provinces. Rome's geographical expansions became synonymous with it religious imperialism, even though spirituality had nothing to do with material belongings. This aggressive spread of the message created a lot of distress, anger and unrest in the new Roman provinces specially the regions of the Arab world, resulting in the formation of a new religion, Islam.

Islam

Islam was founded around 600 CE by Prophet Muhammad, who is revered as the last messenger (prophet) of Allah. Quran, the primary scripture of Islam is believed to be a verbatim record of the teachings of Allah and Prophet Muhammad. Muslims believe that Islam is the complete and universal version of a primordial faith (similar to eternal truth) that was revealed innumerable times before, through many prophets, including Abraham, Moses and Jesus. However, the Arabs of the time refused the preachings of Christianity by refusing to accept Jesus as the 'Son' of Allah as they were completely against idol worship or worship of any form. Their core belief is based on worship of the eternal and not of any manifested creation of the Universe, hence no idols or symbols were ever accepted. Islam, as a religion, became a protection for the Arab population as it united them under a common cause of fighting off the Roman Empire. Some practices such as worshipping the formless nature of God, praying to only one God and offering prayers on a Friday and dilution of the role of the clergy in spiritual pursuits were probably inspired from its affinity to the religious practices followed before Christianity came into existence. In addition, considering everyone as equal, sharing of wisdom with everyone through a holy book and the existence of educational institutions along with places of worship were perhaps few prudent practices of Christianity that were imbibed by Islam. New rules were also fostered. For instance, to counter the rich moneylenders who were primarily Jews at that time, Islam discontinued the practice of money lending for profit thereby removing some of the material imbalances. Further, Islam was the first religion to uplift women, which other religions shunned at the time. Islam gave property rights to a close female relative in the estate of the deceased, as well as allowed widows to remarry anyone they chose. It also treated orphans with respect and encouraged them to be adopted as family members by society. Islam thus corrected many material and spiritual imbalances of the collective wisdom of the time, which led to improvements in the lives of the people, leading to their spiritual liberation at the time.

Awaken From the Past

The Western and Eastern religions were formed to bridge the gap between greater good and the reality of the people in those regions over period of time. They all agreed on the omnipresent and omniscient nature of the Super Soul and to its formless nature. Even in Hinduism, idols are worshipped as avatars and not God in complete existential form. This is to say that the essence of spiritual wisdom has been the same across religions. However, the differences have been caused by the forefathers due to self-glorification and fixation of their own beliefs and practices as best. When we compare these religious practices from a point of seeking, then progress can be made in order to advance one's own journey. However, when we judge across practices then a sense of competition is created which leads to formation of Ego called 'Collective Ego'. Ego is resistance of the self in not letting the spiritual wisdom and energy flow in pure form through you. When we let go of our ego and learn from our past, we can seek wisdom from any religion. With the tools of soulful living, you can instil this eternal wisdom in you and distill the best of all religions for your awakening.

9

LOST IN TRANSLATION-FINDING SPIRITUALITY

Spirituality is based on faith. Words are all we have to describe the spiritual wisdom. To explain this abstract concept, every 'word' used has a special meaning, which is unique to a given context. Sentences communicate more complex thoughts and usually have a wider context. Moreover, a picture has an inbuilt context and can speak a thousand words but lacks the time dimension required for communicating a realization. Therefore, it becomes a challenge to communicate a realization and volumes of texts might be required. Thus, spirituality being multifaceted becomes indescribable and difficult to completely encapsulate it in any form of words or pictures.

Even if one were a great writer like Shakespeare, the real challenge begets from the point of view of the reader. Very few people understand Shakespeare, that too in its original intended way. The process of communication is complete only when the thought is received with the same intent and context as it was sent. All spiritual discourses and religions face this challenge, as their holy texts are not in colloquial (or easy to understand) languages.

Colloquial languages themselves have been subjected to evolution over centuries. In fact, communication is further evolving in the form of limited word counts (like it was on Twitter), acronyms (LOL) and even emoticons. On the other hand, our realizations have evolved with humans carrying out more life activities and experiences leading to a more intense and higher spiritual wisdom. Our yester year's challenge to decode the spiritual wisdom of the scriptures has become more complex today in order to disseminate these new realizations to the current generation of seekers.

Following a guru who can decode such wisdom is one such solution. However, any path chosen should be done with a questioning mind set and a seeker's perspective rather than a believer's. The four tools that increase your spiritual metabolism for soulful living, namely, wisdom, faith, devotion and practice can equip the today's seeker on this self-learning path based on a trial and learning (not error!) method, so no wisdom is lost in translation.

Blind Men and the Truth

Spirituality, as explained by different religions, can be understood from the popular and ancient parable of 'six blind men'. The story is about a group of 'blind' (visually impaired) men who have never come across an elephant before and who learn and conceptualize what it is like by touching it. Each 'blind' man feels and holds a different part of the elephant's body, like a tusk or tail or a leg, and describes it to his 'blind' friends. As they describe the elephant based on their limited vision and experience, their descriptions of the elephant are different from each other and thus incomprehensible. The elephant is akin to the depiction of spirituality and the 'blind' men is a reference to the visually impaired seekers who are blinded by their personal or religious biases and perspectives, and thus the truth is lost in their communication.

Can we understand spirituality in the same (or perhaps in a better) way as our forefathers understood? Is spiritual wisdom locked in ancient texts and words, and thus unattainable or only communicable by its custodians?

Wisdom Of Story Telling

Spirituality cannot be a victim of mere words, sentences, pictures or biases of its preachers. The spiritual science transcends all personal biases alike, irrespective of the region, language and religion.

One of the ways mankind has tried to communicate the essence of realizations is through storytelling. Almost all the Upanishads or holy texts are a compilation of stories communicating certain facets of spiritual wisdom. The Ramayana, Mahabharata and even Bhagavad Purana, in addition to the texts of the Abrahamic religions about Adam and Eve, Noah's Ark and Moses are all conveyed as stories for imparting wisdom. Many dimensions get uncovered in a story that are relevant for a soulprint. Stories, including great literary works, help understand various perspectives of human behaviour in great depth. Plays and movies are modern ways of storytelling and go a long way if one was to consider them from a spiritual perspective. For instance, you identify with certain characters in a movie when you put yourself in their shoes and realize the truth of the choices they face. When you watch it from a soulful perspective, you increase your realizations on possibilities of truth and enrich your life.

Wisdom in Words

Apart from storytelling, the other method to realize spiritual wisdom is to try and seek the truth by going deeper into the context and intentions of the words used in the religious or the holy texts.

The deeper you go, the more meaningful these words become. At the deepest level, you will realize that all words are pointing to the eternal truth and that the same truth is being communicated by different words! For instance, the word 'Bible' comes from the word 'biblio' meaning 'The Book', Bhagavad Gita comes from the words 'Bhag+vad+Gita' meaning 'The Song of God', Quran means 'The Recital', the word 'Torah' in Judaism means 'To Instruct, The Doctrine, The Law'. The titles might seem different on the first glance but they all refer to a compilation of spiritual wisdom and in essence they are saying the same thing, that is, 'a book on spiritual wisdom'. The nature of seeking the common truth is the way towards soulful living.

As a seeker, you should understand a few of the basic words for decoding any spiritual discourse. Foremost are the words used to define 'God' or the 'Super Soul' like 'the creator', 'Bhagawan', 'Lord', 'Allah', 'Adonai', 'Pure Consciousness', 'Supreme Being', 'The Universe' and 'Almighty'.

Words used to refer to the creation are the 'cosmos', the 'brahmaan', the 'world', 'the manifested reality', 'srishti' and 'qayanaat'. All of such words for creation refer to the manifested or the material world around us. A few texts consider the created world to be an indivisible part of the 'creator'. Other words used to refer to the 'soul' are the 'Atma', the 'Eternal Self', Jin, Ruh, the Spirit and the Holy Spirit.

Spirituality pertains to the science and the art of the 'spirit realm'. Similarly, 'spiritual wisdom' refers to a soul's realizations and its magnitude of realizations is referred to as 'consciousness'. 'Being' is also a word that is used both as a verb and a noun. 'Being' comes from the word 'to be' and is a non-active verb. Non-active is not the same as inactive. This means that the act of just 'being', that is, sitting idle in awareness, which is also construed as a soulful activity. The soul's purpose is to just 'be' and to realize and to observe. The word 'being' used as a noun refers to a complete body with soul in it as used in the context of 'a living being'.

One other reference in the texts pertains to the material world as outer world and the spiritual world as inner world. When one world does not progress in relation to the other, an imbalance is created as witnessed in the advent of many religions in the history of spiritual evolution. With subsequent correction in the collective mind-set of the society the balance is restored and peace is maintained in both the worlds. In essence, any one world cannot exist without the other.

Gender in Spirituality

The other aspect of understanding any spiritual discourse is to look past the gender bias in the texts. The truth itself about spirituality is not gender biased. The custodians of the truth or the hitherto seekers and the writers of religious texts have been predominantly male, hence unfortunately the majority of the referential words and interpretations have been male centric. It will take more female seekers and gender unbiased spiritual leaders to tilt the balance of these cultural misinterpretations in favour of the female gender.

In context of gender, it is interesting to note that the two genders are opposite yet complimentary forces that together create the balanced cosmos. This is referred to as the yin and the yang in the Chinese tradition. The yin and yang are the two complementary forces working in unison for the purpose of the creation. One side provides the seed and the other side the construct or the soil for its manifestation. The two forces are equal in importance but perform the purpose that is specific to their context. At certain times, the female side of the equation becomes more relevant to complete the cosmos and at other times the male side takes the lead. Just like the binary code consisting of zeros and ones both female and male forces create the cosmos. Thus the relevance of gender is neutral at the outset. For instance, in Krishna Bhakti, the idol of Radha and Krishna is one, that is, one half of the idol is depicted as Radha and the other half as Krishna, implying that the union is a complete divinity. Even in Shiv Bhakti, the idol of 'Ardhnarishwar' is a depiction of Shiv and Shakti, as half male and half female human form split down the middle. The Million-Realization learning in your journey is that you need to realize the truth from perspectives of both the genders and not limit yourself to the perspective you are born with or the viewpoint that you might acquire on reading of any such text, including this book.

However, when we delve deeper into our awakening, we find that in Hinduism a distinction is clearly made in the classification of the female's role from, that of the male in the functioning of the cosmos. The soul's role as an impregnator of thought is referred to as male, whereas, cosmos's place of being impregnated has been referred to as female. In this distinction, the creator or the Super Soul is always referred to as the male form and called Bhagawan, whereas the material or the manifested world is always referred to as the female form or Srishti. Thus, the seed thoughts are attributed to the male side, and the cosmic abundance or wealth required for such creation is depicted as the female side. The references to female controlled abundances are revered in the many forms of Goddesses such as Goddess Lakshmi (the Goddess of wealth) or as Goddess Saraswati (the Goddess of knowledge). In the spiritual world, the creator or the soul is the most important dot, whereas in the material world the created aspect or the wealth is paramount. No world can function without the other. Both the worlds have to be in sync with each other for any spiritual evolution, hence both female and male sides are equally important.

Ego and Spirituality

When you live without awareness of the soul, that is, without compassion, love and mercy, you base all your decisions and actions out of your intellect or ego. One person's ego snowballs into the 'collective ego' of a group. This means, a group of people or community or society start to believe in their superiority and collectively work from a self-satisfying (or selfish) perspective rather than a universal perspective. A soulful perspective is universal in nature, that is, we all are equal in the eyes of the Universe! Common forms of collective ego can be seen around us as religious ego forms into fanaticism, countryman ego into jingoism, ego of one's race into racism and even ego in belonging to a certain lineage of ancestors into heritage ego or caste ego. Ego in collective forms is more regressive as it spoils generations of collective progress and interrupts the evolution of spirituality of any soulprint born into that community even before one is born into the world. When you receive and impart your spiritual wisdom from the perspective of your ego, the essence of spirituality gets lost. For instance, when you decide to donate to only 'your community' when there are other more needy people in the world, or try to convert seekers to 'your religion', you perpetuate religious ego in these actions. Spirituality is about spreading light of wisdom to those who are seeking it or are living in ignorance, irrespective of their colour, caste, creed, country or religion. If you can see the goodness in others and inculcate those thoughts into yourself then you can transcend your ego and create a higher path of soulful living.

Soulfulness: A Win-Win Proposition

Soulfulness is not a zero sum game but a win-win proposition for the giver and the receiver. The more you illumine your soul, the more inclined you are to spread light all around. Spirituality in the form of religion has spread light over thousands of years of human history. However, spiritual ignorance has also played an important role in the destruction of mankind in the form of religious infightings as experienced in the dark ages. It is critical *to live by using spiritual wisdom, not to die because of it.* Despite of its drawbacks, formation of a religion has been requirement of the times and encouraged new ideologies, new social order and rewritten out-dated and regressive laws and brought in new spiritual revolution that contributed to the development of the collective spiritual body over time.

We are in a fortunate position in the present times that we have access to immense information, much more than any of our previous generations. Today many books are printed in various formats for mass consumption. The Internet brings both width and a certain depth of knowledge sought by any seeker. There has been seamless inter-border movement of information, which makes the world seem 'flat' once again! Mankind has embraced cosmopolitan views with more openness than before as a new way of life. People have become culturally, linguistically and commercially more tolerant and accepting of each other as compared to the history of mankind. Therefore, the world collectively is already at a higher state of being in spiritual wisdom and intelligence than any of the previous generations. There is hope for faster evolution and for lesser loss of wisdom in its translation and distribution because of the technological advancements.

When we connect the dots of religious thinking over centuries of events, we can distill out the essence of spirituality and perhaps true intentions of the seed thoughts directing them. However, when we get fixated on archaic thoughts without logic we become inflexible and regressive, implying that we do not want to seek but follow. *We need to lead our lives into the future and not follow it into the past.* The essence of spirituality becomes the nectar for the seekers and provides the basis for moving ahead on their spiritual quest. Without religious ego, the possibilities of inter-religious learning are immense as everyone will collectively work for spiritual evolution. In the quest for soulful living and learning from the best practices, it is important to be aware of the history and at the same time to not loose out on its evolution for the future on account of its translation!

10

UNITY IN DIVINITY

Where does the spiritual realm begins? Who or what is God or the Super Soul? Does God even exist, or is it a figment of our imagination? What does he or she really look like? These are some of the Million-Realization Questions that mankind has been asking for over thousands of years. Different answers to these questions have led to the creation of different Gods. History is witness to the fact that whenever there is a substantial increase in knowledge and wisdom, our understanding of God evolves. For instance, we have come a long way from the Vedic times where mere uncertainty in the form of torrential rains, thunder, cyclonic winds, forest fires, etc. were attributed to different Gods. And many of the earlier Gods have fallen out of favour due to this evolution of our wisdom. The 21st century has seen unprecedented intellectual development and availability of limitless knowledge in seeking the truth. With the spread of personal computing and Internet, the collective wisdom has increased. The time has come to further evolve our understanding of God, as we know it.

Existence of God

Broadly, history has classified seekers into two spiritual groups: theists and atheists, based on their views on God. Theists are the believers of God. However, religious custodians misbrand 'atheists' as the 'non-believers' whereas they are merely 'non-believers of the Gods of the custodians'. Religions brand agnosticism (people who hold the view that existence of God is unknown or unknowable) as atheism (people who do not believe in *my* God). However, many irreligious people, including doctors and scientists, believe in the presence of a higher power as a source of energy, who can be called seekers of spirituality and are yet to be christened by mankind.

Amongst the organised religious believers there is difference in the understanding of God. Many worship God as a formed existence (idol or deity) and others worship it as a formless existence. Surprisingly, even the idol worshippers, like the Hindus, believe that God is omnipresent and that the idol is nothing more than an incarnation of the higher power, which in essence is formless in nature. *To summarize, everyone believes that there is a higher power, which is omnipresent, omniscient and omnipotent.*

Advaita And Dvaita Schools of Thought

The second aspect of God that has been debated over centuries, is whether God exists as one complete being or is he or she divided into two separate parts, meaning that there are two different aspects of God one as a creator and other as a creation. The Vedas describe the *un*divided nature of God as '*a*dvaita' and the *d*ivided nature of God as '*d*vaita'. The believers of the undivided state of God believe in the creator and the created as ONE single whole. In the advaita school of thought, God is explained as the creator and the created as one or *the subject and the object of an action being one complete whole.*

The believers of the dual or the dvaita state of God believe in the creator and the created as two separate identities. In the Dvaita school of thought, God is the creator, as the subject, and the cosmos or the material world or the physical reality, is *the object.* Hence, there is a separation between the subject and the object. In essence, the cosmos has been created and since something is done, there must be a doer or a creator behind the action. In this belief the creator exists because of the existence of creation as its evidence.

It is implied that only life can create life. Therefore to create the cosmos with life, some higher life form must exist. The cosmos is disciplined and exists in an orderly fashion and is called a 'universe' meaning 'one vibration' of thought. *Thus, the creator precedes the creation and we can marvel at the creation (such as Planet Earth) as the creator's choice of existence.*

The Million-Realization Learning

The earth is *a living being* in the Solar System is the first realization for any spiritual seeker. Just as human beings stand out among all the living beings on this planet, the earth stands out among all the planets. The earth is the 'blue-eyed child' of the one big celestial family of the sun. Although the earth doesn't have a human form but it has a beautiful spherical shape. It does not talk or walk like humans, but it does have its own vibrations and moves on it's orbit. Due to these existential differences, humans find it difficult to accept the earth as a *superior living being.* This predicament is similar to (say) a snake's perspective, which might think that humans are non-living, as they do not look, walk or eat like it! If this logic is accepted, then any life form will be unable to fathom the reality of a higher being just because it does not look or behave like itself. The realization that life and soul can manifest into any shape, size or system of being is a million-realization learning.

Earth As a Living Being

The Earth has a similar constitution to that of a human body. The Earth has approximately 70 per cent of water content and so does a human body. The earth is moving—rotating, tilting, revolving—with its own internal life force just as humans walk, talk, etc. As humans procreate life, so does the earth as nothing dead can nurture life! The Earth is the progenitor of life as life springs from its soil, water and air. The Earth absorbs energy from the sun and so do all the living beings on it. The Earth has a life span of four billion years in comparison to the human life span of maximum 100 odd years. The human race is the 'newest' addition to the planet with just thousands of years of evolution. Thus, planet Earth is a living being having far more power, intelligence and consciousness than the human species. The closer you are to planet Earth, the closer you connect to the higher consciousness or God.

The Earth's soul, intelligence and body are working in unison. They form one complete balanced system called the ecosystem. The Earth in this state is performing all its actions such as gravity, air and water currents, cloud formations, rains, forest growths, and volcanoes. The actions of the Earth comes from its own intelligence and we call them 'Nature' or 'Natural'. One might argue that it is the 'science' of things that drives these forces, but then what is the science in itself and who came up with its rules? Why is the science of gravity on Earth different from that on the moon? The natural law on Earth is specific to Earth itself as it is based on its body and wisdom.

Just like humans have five senses, comparably Planet Earth has her own five sensors—air, water, fire, ether and earth. Based on the sense of pressure, temperature, humidity, sunlight and gravity, Earth directs its actions and energy flows. Earthquakes, hurricanes, climate control, landslides, forest fires, melting glaciers, famines, etc., are called natural disasters. But how can anything 'natural' or 'act of

God' be a 'disaster'? It could be a natural disaster for the human species, but it has a higher purpose and achieves balance for Earth itself. The Earth's spiritual wisdom and intelligence is working all around us and has its own way of maintaining its balance based on its multidimensional sensors. Our understanding of 'acts of God' is limited to our intelligence and our self-interests.

When you want to connect with the higher power who should you connect with—the creator or the creation? Do you connect with the Super Soul (as a creator, formless) or you connect with Planet Earth (as created, formed) or you connect both in matter and spirit (as one complete being)? The answer lies when we go deeper into the realization that the Earth is a complete living being consisting of a soul, intellect, emotive self and a physical body.

The Hindu Trilogy

The Hindu trilogy of Gods includes Lord Brahma, Lord Vishnu and Lord Shiva. Along the way, Lord Brahma fell out of favour and Lord Vishnu and Lord Shiva became the dominant deities. As our understanding and vision expanded, so did our encapsulation of God or the Super Soul. Many wonder about the difference between Lord Vishnu and Lord Shiva and who is superior of the two? This question forms the fundamental way of how we seek God?

Lord Shiva

According to Hindu beliefs, Lord Shiva resides on Kailash Parvat (Mt Kailash) in the Himalayas and has been on Earth since its creation. He is in a state of Samadhi, half-conscious and half-meditative state, and controls all the workings of the planet. He has been instrumental in gifting water to the people of the subcontinent by capturing the holy river Ganga in his hair at the time of its creation thereby symbolically giving life's most important element (water) to the region. His consort is Goddess Parvati, also called Goddess Durga, eponymously meaning 'the guardian of the fortress' (that is, Planet Earth) and has ordained many names based on her powers for building the cosmos.

Lord Shiva has two opposite personalities of his existence, as understood by the Hindu philosophy. One is that of *Bholenath,* or the house dweller, where he has a family with children and also treats animals as his housemates. In this docile personality, he is a nourisher, a disciplined member of the family and also the most merciful one and fulfils the wishes of anyone who prays to him. The other personality of Lord Shiva's is that of 'Rudra'or the hermit like existence, in which he is revered as the most fearless, ruthless and merciless and if anyone goes against his set rules, he strikes balance with one blow. In this form, Lord Shiva is wild in nature and has an independent exploratory life.

In both these personalities of Lord Shiva, we find astonishing similarities between him and Planet Earth. The Earth, too, acts merciful in its bounties and abundance but also strikes a balance with a 'natural disaster' when imbalance is created. The Earth has both a wild as well as an orderly way of existence. Thus, Lord Shiva is a complete being with soul, intelligence and form just like Planet Earth.

Lord Vishnu

Lord Vishnu, on the other hand, does not reside on Earth and is believed to have an abode either in the oceans or in the clouds. He is formless in his existence and lives on earth through his incarnations called 'swarups' meaning 'the self manifested form'. According to Hindu scriptures, Lord Vishnu has incarnated himself as matsya (fish), kurma (tortoise) varaha (boar), Narasimha (half-lion and a half-human), Vamana (dwarf Brahmin), Parashurama (a sage), Lord Rama, Lord Krishna, Buddha and Kalki (yet to be born). His various avatars connote the multi-dimensional possibilities of existence of the higher power. Lord Vishnu is revered as a compassionate power and has manifested as various living beings to achieve a soulful balance in place of imbalance so created due to ignorance or ego of mankind. All the avatars (created form) have a purpose of achieving the balance of righteousness over evil for a higher world order relevant to that time and place. Lord Vishnu is the Super Soul (the creator), who created the Universe through its manifestations for evolution and is a caretaker for natural growth of the collective consciousness in the world.

Lord Brahma's Fall from Grace

Who do you connect with when you connect with God? The advaita form of God as that of Lord Shiva or the dvaita form of God as that of Lord Vishnu? Who should you focus on for spiritual bliss, Lord Vishnu (the creator, the Universe) or Lord Shiva (the complete creation, Planet Earth)?

There is a lovely mythological story that will help to answer these questions. Once Lord Shiva, Lord Vishnu and Lord Brahma were discussing the vastness of the Universe. Lord Shiva, in his wisdom, said that the vastness of the Universe is unfathomable by us as it is formless in nature, whereas Lord Brahma disagreed stating that no creation (or physical matter) can be limitless *and hence* the true creator of that 'limited' cosmos will also be limited in its existence. Lord Shiva took the discussion as a challenge and put his spear down, perpendicular to the ground extending it in both directions 'limitlessly'. Lord Shiva challenged Lord Brahma to try and find any end of the spear and if he succeeds, then the answer to the limited nature of the Universe shall be settled in Lord Brahma's favour. To settle the argument, Lord Brahma followed Shiva's spear into the Universe as far as he could go and see, and Lord Vishnu followed him out of curiosity. Soon, Lord Vishnu returned and admitted that the Universe is *limitless to the best of our understanding*. However, Lord Brahma just to win the argument returned and lied that he had found one end of the spear! This angered Lord Shiva, as the challenge was a way to explain the concept of limitless, and the lie, in essence, falsely questioned pure wisdom. He revealed the wisdom and cursed Lord Brahma of falling out of favour, as a Super Soul would never lie, or act out of ignorance.

Lord Shiva revealed that his spear extended into a circular circuit of an unfathomable size and hence limitless from their perspective. All circles are made up of dots that appear as straight lines at minute levels. The dots seem like straight lines to an ant or human walking on it for eternity. Lord Shiva's spear extended into such a vast circle that it would seem limitless to say an ant or a human travelling along it. Limitless, timeless, immortality and infinity are based on concept of relativity with respect to the person seeking it. Thus Lord Shiva's spear seemed limited to Lord Brahma's ignorance but unlimited from Lord Vishnu's wisdom. Similarly, our understanding of God can be unlimited if we are seeking wisdom or limited if we are following ignorance.

Timelessness is immortality. All Gods and demigods are 'immortals' for humans. Human spiritual wisdom has evolved barely 8,000-10,000 years ago whereas the Earth's wisdom is over 4 billion years old and the Universe's wisdom is estimated at 14 billion years. Hence, we cannot fathom the vastness of Earth's wisdom let alone the Universe's wisdom. For all we know, if the human species does not choose to evolve in its spiritual wisdom and alignment with the higher power, then Planet Earth might replace it with other beings with higher spiritual wisdom.

Connect to Your Super Soul

Your horizon changes as you move from one point to the next. Your horizon also increases in scope as you go 'higher'. Likewise your understanding of God changes as you evolve and as you see yourself in a larger spiritual context. When you increase your vision, you realize that all realities converge into one 'uni-verse' and all parts of the Universe are connected with each other. As the master of your body is your soul, similarly the master of the Earth's activities is the Earth's soul and the master of the cosmos is the Super Soul. All beings on Earth are part of the Earth's soul and it calls to reason that the Earth's soul is in turn connected to the Super Soul or the Universe in the spiritual realm. In this way, when you connect with the Earth's soul then you automatically connect with the Super Soul and vice versa.

When you choose to pray to Lord Shiva (or Planet Earth), or to Lord Vishnu (Super Soul), you connect to the one and the same source of energy as both are connected to each other. You are only making a choice based on your vision and understanding of God, and either ways you are connecting to the same centre of the Universe. All the energies converge in the Universe and in essence direct us towards fulfilling our higher common purpose. The word 'Super Soul' can mean different things to different believers based out of their different limited visions. The believers would tirelessly debate and waste time in convincing others that their understanding of God is better or perfect rather than focus on moving ahead on their soulful path.

Connecting to Lord Shiva or connecting to Lord Vishnu is one and the same spiritual connect. The connection is just like that of the concentric circles, which have all their centres aligned and connected at one epicenter. When you align with any one centre as per your horizon, you align with the higher ones simultaneously, that is, when you connect with the Universe directly and align yourself with it, then you get aligned to the Earth's spiritual centre as well. Like a Matryoshka doll, the definition of the Super Soul keeps expanding and shrinking with our wisdom and ignorance. Do not seek to understand the vastness, form or the duality of the Super Soul but *seek the tools to align your centre (soul) with the existence of the higher power. You can be evolutionary in your understanding of God, and learn that life's journey to seek spiritual wisdom is in fact its destination.* This way, you will spiritually connect to all the Gods as the centre of all the circles of existence, *the Super Soul,* lies inside you!

You need to know the horizon of your soulprint and you need to align yourself with it. Once you seek what your soulprint is comfortable seeing and believing then you can start connecting to it. When you connect to your horizon of the higher power, then you become an e*mbodied soul. In this connect* you get access to limitless spiritual wisdom and power to achieve whatever your soulprint aspires. When we chant, 'Om shanti, shanti shanti' perhaps we pray for complete balance in the form of peace in the three worlds. One 'peace' is for us, the other 'peace' is for Planet Earth and the final 'peace' is for the Universe.

11

GET READY TO CONNECT TO THE SUPER SOUL

On your spiritual journey so far, you have discovered where mankind has been (history) and with whom it needs to connect, that is, understanding of the higher power. Now it is important to understand the nature and flow of energy when you connect with the Super Soul. As you have discovered the importance of the connections of your inner dots, similarly it is important to understand the science and wisdom behind how to connect to the Super Soul in order to achieve the state of embodiment.

The material world of a human life is a limited state of existence. However, the spiritual world is limitless. When you connect your self with the Super Soul you experience an unlimited existence. As a fruit grows to ripen on a tree, comparably a soul attains complete spiritual wisdom only when it is connected to the Super Soul. As your knowledge increases, your intelligence becomes better and as your intelligence increases your living becomes better; however, as your spiritual wisdom grows, your life become better. The connection of the self with the Super Soul is a complete transformation of your existence, where you do not seek to change the rules of your ecosystem, but have the power to change the ecosystem itself!

Tat Tvam Asi (That Art Thou)

In the Vedas, the essence of embodiment is encapsulated in the Mahakavya (the Great Saying of the Upanishads) '*Tat Tvam Asi*' or 'That Art Thou'. Many people misinterpret this and assume that it means 'you are it' or 'you are God', which is misleading. For instance, a tree connected to the ecosystem is an integral part of the ecosystem but not the ecosystem itself! The conjugation of these three words means that '*you and the God are connected as one*'. 'Tat' signifies the eternal truth or the 'Super Soul' (God), 'tvam' refers to your complete self with all the five inner dots and 'asi' refers to the English verb 'is', signifying connection. Thus, the Mahakavya clarifies that a soulprint and the Super Soul are two separate identities, which can be connected in unison to form one unit. This state of connectedness is the embodiment state. The word 'embodied' comes from the words 'em' and 'body' meaning 'connected body'. Like a person in love, who only *knows and feels* the pulse of its connection with the beloved, in the same way only the embodied soul is aware of its connection with the Super Soul.

Upgrade Your Spiritual Wisdom

You might wonder that since you are part of the Super Soul then what is the need to connect to it as you must be already connected to it right from your birth? Your connection to the Super Soul is similar to your connection to the other souls around you. *Any relationship is formed only when you work on it* and interact with the other person in a harmonious way to exchange energy, knowledge, wisdom and emotions. No relationship should be taken for granted lest you want to lose it.

Spiritual connections are like Internet connections, so you have to 'search' (seek) to connect with the source and maintain the connection. Your inner 'software' in terms of spiritual wisdom, faith, devotion and practice needs to be upgraded from time to time to maintain higher connecting speeds of your evolving soulprint. Once connected, the two connected 'devices' can experience the flow of energy. The whole purpose of your spiritual journey is to upgrade your spiritual wisdom from 3G to 4G to 5G to eventually infinite Generation.

Bypass The Spiritual Gatekeepers

It is impossible to ascertain from the outside whether or not a soulprint is an embodied one. To circumvent this challenge, religions, in their own wisdom, have laid down certain norms, rituals and culture, including a dress code, prescribed daily routines, etc. for people who are assumed to be embodied. People who follow these prescribed 'codes' are called priests, pundits, rabbis, monks, maulvis or other saints to distinguish them from the *non-embodied* souls as per their religious wisdom. It would have been more fruitful if the focus from outer presentation could have been made towards focusing to ascertain their awakening. For instance, doctors have to undergo years of education and training before they can practice. This is true for almost every profession except the profession of the spiritual stewardship.

Spiritual (or religious) custodians need to be sieved out to ascertain the depth of their realizations. However, religions usually forbid the believers from going outside the scope of the scriptures and hence limit both the custodians and the followers to seek further. Such static tenets result in the blind leading the blind, and thus spreads ignorance. Due to this ignorance when the followers do not get the results that they have been seeking, they feel shortchanged by the spiritual custodians and are left disappointed with their spiritual practice or religion. This exploitation has been carrying on for centuries as the religions have held spiritual monopoly over their followers. These so-called custodians do more disservice and harm, than good in the society. Selling fake spirituality is more harmful than selling fake medicines, as medicines only affect your body but spirituality influences your soul and transcends all facets of your life.

Once Kabir, a merchant, stumbled upon a genie lamp. On rubbing the lamp, the genie appeared. The genie asked in his loud deep voice, 'What can I do for you?'. The merchant always thought of ways to make money. He asked the genie to make him an Embodied Soul so he can fulfil everyone's wishes around him by praying for them. The genie agreed but enquired the reason behind such an odd request. Kabir replied, 'I want to earn lots of money and with embodiment I can make money for others and take a commission for myself!' The genie laughed as the merchant could have directly asked for money in the first place if that is what he was seeking! When a custodian 'sells' his services, for money, to a fellow soul with the promise to conduct prayers in the hope to make the other's life more prosperous, then this thought is laughable too.

What is even stranger is that at times the custodians, proclaim themselves to be the conduits between one's soul and the Super Soul. These custodians like to take the middle position between one's conversations with God and become the spiritual loudspeakers for the seekers. This aspect is as preposterous as asking someone to exercise on your behalf! Embodiment does not require any middleman or outside interventions.

However, the role of the custodians can be useful as spiritual coaches to others in their spiritual journey rather than becoming gatekeepers for the doors of 'heaven', if there is such a place. A custodian should share their realizations, experiences and wisdom that might guide the seeker. Any seeker can connect to an embodied soul and be, in effect, connected to the Universe. But when you can connect directly in an unlimited way directly to the Universe then to subscribe to a secondary connection (spiritual guru) might not be your first choice. You should place more power and focus on your inner dots to connect with the higher power and at the same time seek guidance from all spiritual gurus as the way forward.

Guru's Role

The word 'guru' comes from the word 'gu' meaning 'darkness' and 'ru' meaning 'destroyer', that is, 'the remover of darkness'. Spirituality is both a science and an art that needs teaching. A real guru can hold your hand in your spiritual infancy and teach you how to walk in your journey. A real guru is pure and selfless in his teachings.

Guru can be either an inner or an outer source of light to remove your darkness. The inner guru is like an engineer who works closely with you on your inner engineering to fix your inner light bulbs of wisdom. He is focused on teaching you *how to fish*, rather than *feed you a fish* once. Such gurus were very popular in the Vedic times as they spent quality time with their disciples. This way, the guru wins your trust and guides you to strengthen your spiritual wisdom and faith. Once you are awakened then you can seek your own path, just as a person who walks in a dark forest with a torch light. On the other hand, the outer guru is like the sun, who shines his wisdom (light) on all-alike and it is up to the soulprint to absorb what it truly seeks. The outer guru, reaches out more to the soulprints who believe in Do It Yourself (DIY) kind of seeking.

A guru has to walk on his own path of spiritual evolution and at the same time, spend time to guide others. So, when you find a guru who is not only unbiased but sacrifices his journey for your awakening, then you need to be truly grateful to him or her and the Universe for connecting you with them. Attaining the balance between self-maximization and selflessness is a Million-Realization learning of a pious guru who is walking on the path of soulful living.

Gautama Buddha professed everyone to walk on the path of enlightenment while fulfilling his or her social and familial responsibilities. Thus, in essence, an embodied soul can be from any worldly profession viz., carpenter, preacher, teacher, businessman, saint, or a pundit. Embodiment is not a profession or a legacy or hereditary in nature. Embodiment is not a privilege by birth, but a choice that an individual makes once he starts on the journey of awakening his soulprint. All soulprints are equally important in the spiritual realm and differ only in their consciousness.

One of the roles of a custodian of a religion is towards the administration and management of the religious places and of the religion itself. The importance of the role of religious clergy comes from selfless management, storage and retrieval of the wisdom accumulated over centuries of spiritual evolution by various soulprints. However, the caveat to this role is that anyone who is a religious head should not make their opinions equivalent to the divine and their proclamations should not be considered the word of God by the believers.

How to Connect to the Higher Power

Embodiment is an experiential space and you have to walk on the path to realize it in your evolution. Before you seek embodiment, you need to make yourself ready for the connection. You might think you are ready, but without the right mental and emotive *software* your efforts will not be effective. First and foremost for embodiment, you need to carry out your *inner purification,* that is, clearing of your inner dots. Only after clearing and purifying your inner space, you will be ready to receive new energies from outside. To invite someone to sit on the chair, you need to first get up and vacate it. There are many ways to purify your self. For instance, Pranayam or deep breathing purifies the breath. Love purifies feelings or the emotive dot. Knowledge and concentration purifies the intellect. 'Seva' or service to others purifies the ego. Meditation and silence purify the soul. Donation purifies the body dot or the material wealth.

After purification, you need to ensure that your *faith in the higher power is intact.* Without faith, in the existence of the Super Soul, how can you connect with it? Without a vision of where you want to go or whom you want to connect with, it becomes impossible to reach there. Knowing the existence of your soul should give you faith in the existence of a larger soul. Each person has his own reasons for keeping faith and this can neither be taught nor transferred from one to other. Faith is different from blind faith as when you walk in a dark forest with a torchlight (faith), you still need to walk with your eyes and ears wide open (rationality).

Apart from keeping faith, gratitude towards the Universe should be your attitude. When you are 'thankful', you exude a positive vibe. State of gratitude comes from the feeling of reciprocation to the benevolent acts already done by the Universe towards your existence. This alignment with the Universe fills the seeker with positive energy for further connection. In a normal business (intellect based) transaction, there is no need for gratitude because 'equal' value is being exchanged in the eyes of the two parties. However, in the limitless spiritual realm, you can never repay or compensate the Universe for its blessings already bestowed on you in form of your life's abundances. You need to aspire and be in a constant state of gratitude towards the Universe.

Even intellectually, when you are in gratitude, it is understood that there are two beings—the giver and the receiver. The receiver has gotten something valuable from the giver and hence the giver is superior to the receiver. Further it is implied that by being grateful or saying the words 'thank you' the cycle of giving and receiving is completed.

Having a feeling of gratitude towards the Super Soul implies that the seeker is happy about their life. When you are genuinely thankful, you are predisposed to return the favour by doing more than what is expected of you, thereby you are open and willing to contribute to the ecosystem at large. If you, the seeker, have not thanked the Universe for all its goodness bestowed on you then the relationship cannot prosper further. Being in gratitude sets the right tone for progress of any relationship. The word 'Upanishad' (upa – ni – shad) means (close-below-sit), that is, the seeker sits closely below the giver of wisdom (as a student). This implies that by placing yourself at par or above the teacher (or giver of wisdom) will not result in any flow of energy (or wisdom) towards you. Thus, state of gratitude towards the Universe sets the proper flow of energy from the Super Soul *downwards* to the seeker.

Lastly, *trust your Intellect*. Intellectual development is required for higher spiritual living as it helps you to decide what you should or should not do. Without having a sense of discernment you will be engulfed in a never-ending loop of your experiences leading you nowhere. Common sense should form the basis of your analytical skills. There should not be any space for blind faith or superstition in your spiritual science. Everything needs to be empirically studied and researched and realized before accepting it as the higher truth at that time. For instance, a few of the religious texts and tenets have been misinterpreted with regard to the truth about the 'revelations of God'. These commandments should not be considered the ultimate truth because someone claim them *to be the words of God*. For the seekers, the context of the spoken truth is as important as the truth itself. Only after realizing the revealed truth by your own self you can evolve your soulprint. This quest is an integral part of soulful living or rational consciousness where you are rational about your beliefs and at the same time trust your intellect when making soulful decisions.

Prayer, Your Spiritual Anchor

Once you are ready to connect, you start building a relation with the Universe through your conversations. *What you seek determines what you should pray.* Generally, there are two kinds of prayers—one is for the overall wellness and the other is for a specific need. Different soulprints seeks differently, hence no prayer can be judged by anyone. For instance, asking for a 'Ferrari' might be just as important to a seeker as a prayer for knowledge to another seeker. However, when you ask for overall wellness then the Universe gives you the best possible solution, probably unfathomable to your intelligence. It is from a higher level of consciousness that you pray for universal well being.

When your prayers get fulfilled, then your ego too has a humbling experience as it sees the higher power at work around it. Up till now, your intellect in the form of your ego was pretty much taking all the credit for the things achieved by the perceptive dots, that is, the emotive and intellect. Your soul's role in your existence gets stronger through this inner bonding of prayers with the Super Soul. On achieving this awakening, more avenues present themselves for your spiritual development, as now you are ready to change yourself as well as the rules of the 'game' by praying for the cosmic blessings. From a state of limited existence of self-absorbed focus, you strive for a limitless canvas to create a better ecosystem for all. The science behind prayers that can help you to communicate better in your conversations with God is discussed in the next chapter.

12

MAKE YOUR LIFE A PRAYER

What is a prayer and does it have any basis in spirituality, or is it just a conversation you think you are having with God? How many times is enough to pray in a day or a week? Is praying in a temple or 'House of God' more effective than praying at home? Are rituals different from prayers? Is it important to pay attention to the language and syntax you use in your conversation with the Universe?

My words fly up, my thoughts remain below,
Words without thoughts, never to heaven go!

Shakespeare (Hamlet)

Man Proposes God Disposes

Prayers were an integral part of mankind even before religions were established. Prayers are the medium through which your thoughts manifest into words, habits and actions. Prayers are conversations between your soul and the Super Soul. All the prerequisites of embodiment, that is, purification of self, faith, gratitude (towards the Super Soul) and trust (in your intelligence) are the starting points of offering a prayer before it is offered to the Universe. Without having the correct syntax, your prayers probably end up becoming a wish or just a musing of the mind.

On the other hand, with proper syntax or vibe, sometimes even silence is the best conversation you can have with anyone. Prayer is a process by which you *till* your body, mind and the intellect, like a fertile piece of land, and then sow seeds of thoughts and ideas into it. These seeds of thoughts once sown await the cosmic *will* to accept and germinate them. Like many seeds planted in the world, many thoughts see the light of the day whereas many fall by the wayside. 'Man proposes and God disposes' means that it is entirely upon the Universe to accept or reject your prayers. This is the reason we 'offer' our prayers and not 'say' them to the Universe.

An important realization is that through prayers, you only offer suggestions to the Super Soul, and the choice to accept them or not lies unilaterally with it. Thus, you should never be disheartened or angry when your prayers are not answered, as you should not confuse *'your will'* with the *'eternal will'*. Eternal *will* has its own intelligence and design for evolution, which may or may not align with your prayers at any given point of time. The onus of such alignment with the higher power is yours and not of the eternal space. Spiritual duty of the self is to do its karma and continue to plant ideas with unattached emotions and expectations. Probably, if all your prayers get answered as per your requests, then you could become haughty and complacent and take miracles for granted.

When you pray, focus on aligning your *will* with what you might consider the eternal *will*. Peace and happiness for everyone around is one such noble prayer that you can focus on while aspiring to align your personal goals. The age old Vedic prayer, 'Vasudhaiva Kutumbakam' is one such realization of treating (aligning with) complete Universe as one's own family.

However, when your prayers are not answered, *you need to prepare your fertile soil again, perhaps with more piety, work on the depth of your seed thought with more compassion and intelligence and then offer new seeds again to the Universe.* You need to water your prayers, that is, channelize your energies into your seed thoughts. When you are well-aligned with the eternal will along with your dedicated focus to make your prayer a reality, then nothing can stop that seed thought from growing to its fullest. Prayers are thus vehicles, through which you put this science of connecting, preparing, tilling and planting of the seed thoughts to the Super Soul, in manifesting a better world for yourself and others.

The Domino Effect of Your Prayer

A small idea in your prayer becomes a thought. Your thoughts become your word. Words become your action. Actions become your habit. Habits become your character. Character becomes your destiny! Your small ideas (or wishes) can lead to bigger manifestations when the cosmic intelligence is aligned with your prayer. This external impetus or 'wind beneath your wings' is based on the realization that you are part of the cosmos and work in unison with it.

When you pray, someone listens! so be careful what you pray for, as it might get answered. This means that all your prayers are coming from your present level of spiritual wisdom. As your spiritual wisdom evolves, you will find your future self present in a manifested reality prayed from the past. This might make your present reality seem redundant with your current evolved aspirations and prayers. For instance, you might have prayed for an investment banker's job at Wall Street only to realize that you do not like the stressful long working hours or your ruthless boss, and start to seek peace and happiness which was actually what you were seeking when you prayed for that job. Hence, you need to always be cognizant and make your prayers bigger by imagining a better universe for yourself and around you.

I do not doubt the self I was,
Was competent to me,
But something awkward in the fit-
Proves that – outgrown–I see-

Emily Dickinson

The Ritual of Praying

How many times can or 'should' you pray in a day? Islam advocates prayers to be offered five times a day to be sufficient, Christianity encourages praying on Sunday as it is the seventh day of creation of the 'Lord God', whereas in Hindu practice of praying is as per individual's wish, ranging from once a week to keeping no count of the number of times one has prayed, which includes zero times! Religions may vary in their prescriptions for the praying timetable but they all believe that it is only by praying one connects with the Super Soul.

Vedic wisdom has given a more universal answer. It states that *we need to be in the embodied state not as a matter of need but as a state of being.* You should make your work your religion and your religion your work. This means you should be in a constant state of equanimity with your self and the cosmos at all times. Your every thought or decision is a prayer in itself and you should live in such piety in your everyday life. When you think, feel and act soulfully then all your wishes are universally accepted and blossom into the world you envision. Any act or thought you do outside the space of your soulfulness does not get the cosmic intelligence, energy or its 'blessings'. Thus, time spent by one on praying can range from no time spent to leading a perpetual soulful life.

Temple Run

What is the purpose of going to places of worship when the conversation with God is between the individual and the Super Soul? Isn't the Super Soul omnipresent? How can a manmade building as a place of worship or an edifice be more relevant for connecting to the Super Soul? These are a few questions that a rational seeker seeks answers to.

The spiritual journey is both an inner and an outer one. When you pray in solitude you strengthen your bonds of embodiment, however, when you pray with others then the collective spiritual bond increases. The purpose of going to a place of worship is for the seeker to reaffirm their belief system with others, and also understand and learn from the experiences of others. Interacting and connecting with other souls can make your faith and devotion stronger.

Another reason for visiting a place of worship is to imbibe the positive vibes of such a place. Such places have a higher magnitude of positive vibes, as everyone in such places is present with a sense of compassion, faith and love for the Super Soul. The older a place, the higher should be its energy levels and positivity around it. It is just like watching a sporting match in a stadium and sitting among people who are cheering for your team. The euphoria is energizing and contagious to say the least.

The third reason is the fact that experiential learning through interactions with other seekers is way better than reading any self-help book. The places of worship in essence are like spiritual fitness centres providing resources like books on faith, lectures, etc., which one might need to further one's spiritual development.

Satsangs (Sermons), prayers, chantings and story-telling sessions are generally held at places of worship and bring about community learning. These places currently may not be what we seek out of them but with the right thought and vision we can create them for our future generations.

The fourth reason to visit places of worship is both profound and scientific at the same time. It is believed that the cosmos is a depiction of the Super Soul; hence the temples are constructed as visual depictions for the seekers to realize this wisdom on their visit.

The Hindu temple architecture tries to capture the inner dots of the human body and its connection to the Super Soul. For example, all temples have a set of stairs at their entrance, connoting the legs of a person, which uplift the structure of the body. After we enter the temple, there are inner shrines to denote the perceptive bodies of our inner world. These precincts lead us to the innermost sanctum called the 'Garbhagriha', meaning the 'womb residence' or the residing place for the soul. Also, the temple's largest feature from the outside is the shikhara or vimana or spire, which is just above its innermost sanctum to reinforce the belief of the soul's connection to the Super Soul. In addition, mostly the ancient temples face towards the east, which further substantiates the inner belief of seeking light or wisdom from the eternal source, that is, the sun or the higher wisdom.

The Lord Shiva temples in India are known for their connection to nature. Each temple has a Shiva linga. The word 'linga' in Sanskrit means 'evidence' or 'proof', and is actually an aniconic depiction of the Super Soul. Interestingly, the Shiva lingams in five temples of South India represent the five elements of nature.

1. In the Ekambareshwarar temple in Kanchipuram, Lord Shiva is represented by a lingam made out of sand to depict the earth element.
2. The Jambukeshwarar Temple in Trichy depicts the water element. In the shrine of the temple, a stream of water flows under the lingam. This engulfs the lingam with water,

embodying the water element.

3. The Arunachaleswarar Temple at the base of Arunachala hills, depicts the fire element with a huge beacon lit atop the hill to symbolize the Shiva lingam.
4. Located on the banks of the Swarnamukhi River, the Kalahastheeshwara Temple depicts the air element. Lord Shiva is worshipped at this temple in the form of Vayu Lingam, representing the wind. There is a lamp inside the inner sanctum that is constantly flickering to confirm the presence of air inside. The Vayu Lingam can be observed to move even when the priests close off the entrance to the main deity room, which does not have any windows!
5. The Thillai Nataraja Temple in Chidambaram worships the ether (sky) element, the subtlest of the five elements. Lord Shiva is worshipped in a formless nature here.

Once you visit such a special place of cosmic energy, you feel more connected with the Super Soul, which is the purpose of your visit. However, in the effort to get to a place, do not lose the purpose of your visit. Whether praying at your home or in a place of worship, your focus towards your embodiment should remain the main reason for the visit, as your inner journey starts before your outer one. After all, your body is also like a temple, for it resides your soul, that is in fact part of the Super Soul.

The Wisdom Behind Rituals

Rituals are the physical actions of your prayers. Prayers are offered in the spiritual realm and rituals are actions in the material realm. While carrying on a ritual all your inner dots must be in unison with your soulful prayer. In this unified exercise, the prayer becomes a complete offering of your body, emotive, intellect and soul. A ritual can be as simple as sitting in a meditative state or joining your hands in posture of namaste.

A ritual can also be complex like performing a yagna, which is an elaborate process in front of a sacred fire. Yagna signifies the sacrifice of one's ego as an offering into the eternal truth, that is, the fire. For a seeker, it is important to understand each and every act performed in a ritual as every detail has a deeper thought. Performing a ritual without seeking the wisdom behind it is as good as doing a physical exercise. Do not perform a ritual blindly, as it is only in seeking that you realize the truth. On the other hand, knowing the complete truth about each and every act of an ancient ritual is a process of seeking and might not dawn on the practitioner in the first instance of performing it. These ancient rituals were enacted by spiritual leaders of the Vedic times after they attained deep realizations and logic for such practices. For a practitioner to realize the same depth of wisdom at the beginning of his journey might be unrealistic. Also, each act might relate to a different realization for the different seekers based on what they are seeking at the time. Hence, as long as you are seeking wisdom in such acts with your eyes open, then you are awakened on your spiritual path.

Master the Art of Prayer

In the same way, when you offer any prayer without knowing it's meaning then it is similar to singing a song in a foreign language and this habit should be avoided. In Hinduism, the original text of prayers were written in Sanskrit, in Buddhism it was written in Pali, in Judaism it was written in Hebrew and in Jainism it was written in Prakrit. All these languages are barely written or spoken today. Christianity (English), Islam (Arabic), Sikhism (Gurumukhi) are a few of the fortunate ones to have their holy spiritual texts in modern languages.

There is a certain merit in reciting a prayer in an ancient language as such prayers have the thoughts beautifully encapsulated in the best way possible. For example, 'Om Namh: Shivay', is sweeter to say than 'Om, the cosmic vibrations, I bow to Lord Shiva!' Irrespective of the language, you must try to understand the meaning, context and the realization that you are seeking at the time of offering a prayer.

No prayer can be classified as best, as each prayer is relevant to a soulprint in its evolution. Many of the ancient popular prayers are general and evergreen in nature, as they come from a soulful self, manifesting for the betterment of everyone. For instance, In Hinduism, the Gayatri Mantra is a request to the Universe asking it to connect with our intellect and soul in order to illumine all our inner dots.

Prayers over centuries of evolution and across religious beliefs, reveal a broad distinct format or syntax that makes up for an effective prayer. The seeker can connect these common dots of prayers offered across religions. The first step of starting a prayer, as mentioned earlier, is to fulfil the four prerequisites of embodiment required to give the right predisposition to the seeker. The second step pertains to the conversation with the Universe and starts from offering appreciation to the Super Soul for its supremacy and benevolence. These are not false praises and should not be said superficially. You need to appreciate acts done by the Universe in your prayers. For instance, following is one of the most popular and revered prayers of Lord Shiva:

Kapurgoram Karunavtaram Sansarsaram Bujgendra Haram, Sada Vastam Hirday Arvindey, Bhavam Bhavani, Sahitam Namami

(You, the Super Soul, is as pure, illumined and revered as camphor; You are the manifestation of compassion; You are the essence of the entire cosmos; You embrace all beings like the garland around your neck; You are the giver of perpetual bliss; I request you to always reside in the lotus of my heart; Oh Lord and Goddess (Sati: wife of Lord Shiva); I bow to you both together.)

This prayer, in essence, praises the unimaginable size and nature of Lord Shiva and his benevolence towards the growth of our spiritual wisdom.

Similarly, in Koran, all verses start with the phrase, 'In the name of Allah, the Compassionate, the Merciful'. This is appreciation of the Super Soul's compassion and mercy. Even in 'Ganesha Vandhana' the prayer for Lord Ganesha, the seeker praises the might and the glorious acts of Lord Ganesha. This is evident in all the beautiful names believers have bestowed on him such as 'Siddhi Vinayak' meaning leader of wisdom, or 'Vighnaharta', meaning remover of obstacles.

After appreciation, we can offer our seed thought as a 'humble request' to the Super Soul. At this point, we are asking the Super Soul to accept our seed thought and let it germinate. We should never judge a prayer for the type of 'request' it submits. Higher realized spiritual bodies would have a broader vision in their prayers. However, for a new seeker, a focused prayer might be better as it solves a very specific challenge they face in their life. Also, when (or if) the prayer gets answered, the seeker can specifically know that it has been answered. This builds upon his faith in the process of praying from a higher level later. There are many Gods and Goddesses in Hinduism for specific needs, for example, Goddess Saraswati is the custodian of knowledge, Goddess Lakshmi of wealth, Lord Ganesha of prosperity.

Souls with higher spiritual wisdom offer prayers for the greater good. When you ask the Super Soul for general well-being, it opens up multi-dimensional possibilities for you. This is true because you do not know everything and thus do not know what is missing in your life. *You know not, what you know not*! Thus it is best to leave the modalities to the Super Soul in your ultimate desire to attain peace and happiness. For example, one's desire to be a wealthy or a famous person, stems out of ignorance that all wealthy or famous people are happy! To fight such ignorance, your prayers need to keep the faith in the Super Soul and believe that the bigger design is always for your betterment and everyone around you!

The Magic of Manifestation

There is an interesting story in the Vishnu Purana of King Hiranyakashyap and Lord Narasimha, which aptly explains the virtues of offering general prayers and having faith in the Super Soul.

Hiranyakashyap was an arrogant king, who self proclaimed himself to be God, as he was given a boon of immortality. His boon protected him from dying in the following circumstances or time, which pretty much covered all possibilities of one's death—he could not die in the daytime or the night-time, neither with chemicals nor weapons, neither inside a house nor outside, neither in the sky nor on the ground, neither by a man nor an animal.

Hiranyakashyap was blessed with a son, Prahlad who was a believer of the Super Soul, Lord Vishnu. Prahlad prayed to the Super Soul for 'betterment of everyone' around him. In such general prayers of Prahlad, the belief in the cosmic intelligence over his own is depicted. Hiranyakashyap, however, was angry about his son's supposed lack of respect for him, so he challenged Prahlad to fight with him and dared him to call Lord Vishnu for his help. Prahald in his last hour of struggle called upon the Universe and Lord Vishnu appeared in the avatar of Lord Narasimha (who was half-man and half-lion). Further, he appeared at twilight hour (neither in day nor at night time). Lord Narasimha grabbed Hiranyakashyap, and dragged him to the entrance door of the house (neither inside nor outside the house), and placed him on his thighs (neither on the ground nor in the sky), and used his long lion nails to tear apart his body (neither chemicals nor weapons). The story brilliantly describes the possibility of manifestation of the unfathomable cosmic intelligence. When you offer prayers for the general well-being of everyone then they will work wonders for you. Prahlad could not have ever imagined the Super Soul in the manifested form of Lord Narasimha, as he was limited in his own understanding and realizations of the Universe's possibilities.

After offering a prayer to the Universe, you need to work on positive affirmations for the prayer to be answered. Like chanting is a way to control the intellect into meditating, similarly reciting affirmations is a way to generate energy around a prayer so that it is manifested. Human speech should not be taken casually as per Vedic wisdom. *Whatever you say has the possibility of coming true provided you are true to it yourself.* If you always speak from a pure heart and never lie, then the cosmic intelligence will always work in your favour to transform your words into reality. In the Vedic times, this was called vak-shakti and believed to be the norm during Satyug (the era of soulful living). The blessings or shraps (curses) of saints, or rishis or munis used to manifest into reality for everyone around them, including the kings. There are many interesting incidents in the Ramayana and Mahabharata that are based on this concept. Likewise, reciting affirmations and sending out positive vibrations into the Universe also help your prayers to manifest into reality.

The next step is to just wait and have patience. Because irrespective of what you think, you might not be ready to receive what you have asked for and not even be aware of this fact. Focus on your realizations and ponder over the real purpose of your prayer. Sometimes it could take a lifetime to have your prayer answered and sometimes it could be instantaneous. Answering a prayer is entirely up to the cosmic intelligence. Never expect your prayers to be answered as it implies that you can dictate the cosmic intelligence. It is just like when you plant a seed, all you can do is just water the soil and hope (pray in this instance) for it to germinate. However, how the buds will grow, how many flowers will bloom, and will they, later, become delicious fruits is not up to you. You need to be like a farmer in your prayers. *Till* the soul and wait. Just like sowing in farming, patience is important for harvesting realizations.

You might argue that if prayers can be answered in this way, then it seems that any physical effort or hard work is not required for your prayers to come true! That thought is an insincere one as when all your actions are done based on soulfulness as described in the Karma, Dhayana, Gyan and Bhakti Yoga, then there is no scope to practice inaction or lethargy. When you truly seek something and pray for it, then all your inner dots do work in unison towards achieving the goal and in that essence your efforts, emotions and intellect perform their roles and duties towards realizing your prayers into reality.

Lastly, gratitude should remain your attitude irrespective of the outcome of your prayer, though an honest prayer is always answered. When and how it will be answered is for the cosmic intelligence to decide. Maybe some are answered in your next lifetimes, after all, cycles of rebirths carry spiritual wisdom from past lifetimes. Moreover, the answer of a prayer can be a 'Yes' or a 'No' or a 'Not Now'. If the answer to your prayer is a 'No' or 'Not now', then have patience because the cosmic intelligence has a better plan for you than you could ever imagine. *Learn to be patient about your impatience*! Cosmic intelligence always works in your best interest, so any answer is a good answer and you should be at peace with yourself and continue to be filled with purity, gratitude, faith and trust so that you can pray further.

Prayers can be out of any level of your consciousness, however, if prayers are soulful then they make a bigger difference in your life. As you move ahead in your spiritual journey, your prayers become more vast and encompassing of the Universe. This is what makes up for the soulprints of truly great and noble people in the world, who are known for their great achievements. Prayers of such soulprints are not only soulful, but also aligned to the cosmic will, aspiring to make the world a better place.

13

BE AWARE OF YOUR THOUGHTS: SOULFUL AND SINFUL

What makes an act soulful or sinful? What makes a thought or an action 'right' or 'wrong'? Who should decide and who actually decides this for us?

Intent of Your Act is Paramount

The word 'volition' comes from a Latin word, 'volo' which means '*will*' or intent. In essence, it means the inner life force of anything. The intention or life force of a thought is called volition. Energy flows from one point to the other and is a three-step process; it has a beginning (starting dot), a direction of flow (intention) and a destination (finishing dot). In simple terms, an idea or a thought(s) leads to an intent(s), an intent(s) leads to an action(s), an action(s) leads to a habit(s), habits leads to a character and characteristics of a person lead to his spiritual growth! Thus, everything you do starts from a thought. But a Million-Realization Question is from where does a thought begins and where does it aspire to go?

The starting point of a thought can be any of the five inner bodies, namely, body dot, life breath dot, emotive dot, intellect dot or the soul dot. This starting point of the thought ascertains its intent, that is, to be either a self-consuming thought or an altruistic one. As thoughts lead to actions, *emotive thoughts result in acts of passion, intellectual thoughts result in acts of ration and soulful thoughts result in acts of compassion.* This means that the same action, on the outside, can be good or bad depending upon where the thought is emanating from inside you. For instance, the thought of building a place of worship for spreading spiritual wisdom is soulful when it endeavours towards spreading compassion, faith and love. However, building it for reasons of religious domination is an egoistic thought as it propagates religious ego and thus deteriorates the society in that ignorance. We can 'judge' a thought as right, wrong, good, bad based on its intent and not by its outcome. It is this inner 'context' that is more important than the result. This fact of results vs. intention is the basic difference between the material world and the spiritual world. *In the material world, the conclusion or the result is most important whereas in the spiritual world the intent or the context is paramount.*

Not all living beings have such spiritual confusion in their minds. For example, grass never feels it has grown in a wrong place or mosquitoes never discriminate among the people they bite. Only humans have the sense to differentiate the right from the wrong owing to their spiritual wisdom. A mother's love for her child is soulful, whereas a mother's blind love for her child is sinful. She can aspire for her children to perform the best or achieve their true potential (soulful). However, her ambition to make her child come first in the class, that is, to do better than other hard working classmates is a misplaced thought in ignorance of her ego (sinful).

For instance, in the Mahabharata, Arjuna's intention on the battlefield is different from Duryodhana's. Arjuna was fighting for the greater good (soulful) whereas Duryodhana was fighting for his ego (sinful), as he did not want to concede 'land even of the size of the tip of the needle' to the Pandavas. Had Duryodhana shown some compassion and acceded to Krishna's suggestion to give five villages to the Pandavas then probably Mahabharata wouldn't have been fought, as righteousness would have been maintained in the society. Likewise, culling a lamb as a family member in order to symbolize it as an offering of utmost self-sacrifice for God has a higher place than culling animals just for fun or taste or acts of thoughtless religious practice! Sacrificing oneself for the greater good, as done by Jesus Christ, is entirely different from a terrorist 'sacrificing' himself by blowing himself up along with innocent bystanders. The difference is not in the act itself (sacrificing oneself) but in its intent, that is, greater good (soulful) vs. religious vendetta (sinful).

Commonly Misunderstood Intentions

To change the world and to be soulful, you first need to change your intentions or inner context of your thoughts. Once you realize this, then you no longer judge an action from its outcome, you develop a deeper understanding of soulful and sinful living. Spiritual wisdom gives the insight to ascertain whether the intention of your thoughts and the resultant actions are well founded or not. *The more soulful you are on the inside, the more pious actions you do* on the outside. For instance, when people give donations with expectations to receive other people's praises in return then it is not an act of compassion but an act of exchange.

Donation vs. Gift

Moreover even acts of non-exchange might not be soulful. For instance, both acts of gifting and donating are intended well and perhaps noble but donations are not gifts and vice versa. In a gift, the *receiver* is an extension of your body sheath whereas in a donation the receiver is an extension of your soulful sheath. For instance, giving money to 'your' children can be called a 'gift' but giving the same to a needy will be construed as donation. Gift is from the giver's intellect dot where they want to garner love or goodwill for self, whereas donation is from a soulful state where they seek to be altruistic towards everyone alike. Usually, the identity of the giver remains visible in a gift whereas in a donation it is absolved. When you 'donate' with the expectation of getting something in return (for your ego dot) then it is a transaction and not an act of philanthropy. Whereas when you donate, the returns add to your realization of 'Vasudhaiva Khumbukam' (the Universe is one big family), and your spiritual wisdom grows. However, both donations and gifts are noble acts which should be done *intelligently.* Soulful intelligence is the path of soulful living.

A few people might argue that what is so wrong in expecting something in return? Why are 'communist' thoughts assumed to be more spiritual than thoughts for personal gain or a capitalist way of life?

'Where' is the intention placed in a capitalist structure (like USA) or a communist structure (like China) is a Million-Realization Question. Capitalism and communism are only economic structures used to allocate resources. In communism, a country becomes the owner collectively and in capitalism, people become the owners individually. The *intent* of both of the structures stays the same, that is, to improve lives of people by providing goods and services in the most efficient and effective manner. The 'head' or the decision maker is a singular master in the capitalist structure and a 'board' or a collective master in a communist structure. History has proven time and again, that privately owned business empires have failed and so have the communist structures, due to unethical (non-soulful) behaviours of the people leading them. *Only if capitalism has its heart in the right place and communism has its head, we can realize the best spiritual outcome of any system.*

Fasting

The effectiveness of fasting depends on its intentions. Many argue that if the human body needs food then why cause it discomfort by denying what it needs, that is, food? The act of fasting might seem regressive, but with the right soulful context you can make it very progressive. Hence, the spiritual wisdom should always accompany all the actions of an awakened soulprint.

Foremost, the purpose of any kind of abstinence is to lead a disciplined life by ensuring that the senses of the body are in control of the intellect, which is in turn in control of the soul. This is more important in present times, when there is more focus on maximization of pleasures and instant gratifications. Fasting is wilful abstinence, not starvation or skipping of meals due to a busy schedule. Thus, intention needs to be one of control of the soul over the intellect and in turn over the body in the form of wilful abstinence. This is the reason, when we finish our religious fasting at the end of the day, we are asked to feed our senses with the abstained item at that time. *Wilful abstinence and wilful consumption together make up for a complete fast cycle.* Wilful abstinence strengthens your willpower, which makes you stronger in being soulful. 'Sacrificing' things that you do not need or like, or things that do not belong to you is not wilful abstinence. Thus, in today's context even 'smartphone fasting', that is, trying to abstain from the use of your smartphone for a prescribed period, is as effective an exercise as any regular fasting of Vedic times. In spiritual science, any kind of fasting is acceptable if it is wilful and done soulfully.

Secondly, the purpose of fasting is to focus (intellect dot) on the spiritual realm rather than the material world. Practices such as Vipassana where an individual gives up speech or communication for a long period of time, enhances one's inner reflection. On its practice, your energy focuses on the inner dots and moves away from the outside interactions. By wilfully taking away your interactions with the outside world, you take long strides in advancing your inner world, especially if you are too absorbed in, or distracted by, the material world.

Thirdly, self-sacrifice increases the compassion (soul dot) of your soulprint. By giving up a necessity for a day, you are able to empathize with the misery of people living in poverty or in deplorable conditions. For example, scarcity of food and water is a sad reality for many people in the world. By experiencing their deficiency for a limited period of time, you increase your realization and perhaps compassion for the other souls around you who are perpetually living in such deficiency. Abstinence gives you the realization to count your blessings that might go unnoticed in your everyday life.

Fourthly, self-sacrifice is a way of penance (the emotive dot). However, sometimes in practice of penance, physical pain and discomfort are misconstrued as legitimate reactions to the wrongful acts done earlier in order to punish the self. This is regressive and should not be practised, *as two wrongs do not make a right*. If you have committed an unjust act, then the best way to offer penance is to first realize the mistake and then do soulful acts to make up for that deficiency, caused by your wrongful act, in the environment.

Lastly, the purpose of the act of abstinence is to cleanse the physical body system (the body dot). When you follow a pattern then breaking it helps to reset the system. All natural cycles are broken once in a while. It is the exceptions that prove the rule and so is true for the complete wellness of your body dot. In a healthy body strong inner dots reside, which bring about a higher soulful living experience.

Repentance

Repentance is another act that different religions interpret differently. The intention behind repentance is that the 'sinner' realizes that they have done a '*non-soulful*' and an irreversible act. Repenting is more than just saying 'sorry', it is to live in the realization that the act done was incorrect and will never be repeated. In repentance, it is the realization of the mistake by the soulprint that is of prime importance.

Purpose for wilful abstinence can be relevant to a seeker depending upon what their soulprint is seeking through that unique act of fasting. Volition, sacrifice, fasting, repentance or any other word or act should be used and practised in the context of soulful intentions. It is the starting point of the thought (soul or intellect), the direction (intention) and the aim (purpose), which makes an act soulful or sinful, thereby making your intention speak for itself. Thus you can change your karma or spiritual vibrations by just changing the volition of your thoughts while carrying on your actions. For example, if you are in the business of cutting trees to make furniture then this non-soulful act has a fundamentally misplaced purpose of *taking away* from the nature. You can fix this problem by planting more trees than you cut which will change your intent towards a higher purpose of *creating more* abundance in the Universe. In this way, the human need for furniture is satisfied and the environment also evolves further. When you are aware of what is the context, intention or purpose of a thought, then you can strengthen your endeavours by making them soulful instead living life in ignorance by carrying out sinful acts. This awakening is the way forward for soulful living!

SECTION 3

ENLIGHTENMENT—BALANCE THE INNER AND THE OUTER WORLDS

14

KNOW WHY YOU ARE HERE

A Million-Realization Question that often comes to our mind is why are we here? Is there a purpose of our being and if so, what is it? Is the power to shape our life in our hands or in the hands of the Super Soul? If everything is predestined then why should we work at all, and if everything is in our hands then what is the importance of the embodiment and prayers to seek the Universe's blessings? What is the significance of rebirth and what if we choose to not believe in it?

Destiny at Work

The Universe or the 'one synchronized system' propagates the theory that everything is in an orderly way. Flow of energy on earth is governed by its rules (or science like physics, chemistry etc.) and so is the soulprint's energy in the spiritual realm. What might seem as random or chaotic to an individual is in perfect harmony to the knower of its truth. For instance, why are few people 'gifted' with talent at birth while others are not! These random events when attributed to destiny might force the soulprint to negate the importance of its own actions. However, spiritual wisdom can enlighten the way out of our ignorance.

When a ball is left at the top of a slope, it rolls down due to the stored energy in it. Similarly, the play of events in our life were set in motion 'even *before we came here*', which we might not remember or realize were set in motion by us. In this way, we are governed by past trajectories called destiny. However, our perspective on destiny is based to suit our intellectual needs. We attribute our success to our intelligence, and our failures to the unknown, external factors especially destiny. However, we attribute other people's success to their destiny and their failures to their ignorance! People, who value their intellect more than soulfulness, negate the existence of destiny. They live their entire life from perspective of the intellect. On the other hand, people rely on their destiny to the fullest and demean the power of their own efforts. One needs to live life in balance of the two forces and see them as part of one holistic perspective to life. Simply put, we have to continuously work hard while going through the flow of events (destiny) of our lives in an unattached way.

To see 'destiny at work', you have to step back and look at the bigger picture around you. When you see things from a macro view then they seem more logical than from a micro view, as spirituality is a much bigger canvas. As you deal with a bigger ecosystem, you see a better and more efficient pattern, which works out for everyone. For instance, the traffic light system might stop you from rushing to fulfil your urgent work commitments and might seem inefficient at an individual level, but collectively it works wonderfully for everyone alike. The five inner bodies of the self constitute the five collective ecosystem or collective bodies such as, the Super Soul, collective intelligence, collective emotive dot, collective life breath and collective physical space. From the macro viewpoint, the five collective bodies work just as an individual works in a micro perspective. The collective sheaths work in greater expanse and over longer time periods. These collective flows are experienced as *destiny at work* by a soulprint.

Newton's Law in the Spiritual Realm

What you give to the Universe, it reverberates back to you. Every action has an equal and opposite reaction at physical as well as at spiritual level. These reactions are present at the individual level as well as the collective level. When a drop of water falls on a still water body, a ripple is formed, that is, your individual actions vibrate across the collective body, and similarly the actions of others have an effect on you.

When you enrich your individual self, then all the collective bodies around you also get enriched and vice-versa. All great souls have not only enriched themselves but also the collective body around them. A yogi enriches the collective spiritual wisdom, a businessman enriches the collective wealth, an artist enriches the collective emotive body, and a fitness trainer enriches the collective fitness and so on. This means that your inner bodies are interrelated to the five inner bodies of everyone around you! When you are happy, you spread happiness all around. And when you have material wealth, you (ought to) spread wealth around as well! When you plant trees, even for yourself, then people around you also get fresh air. Whatever actions you do for yourself, you, in effect also do for the collective body. Such collective wealth takes longer to be created and also lasts longer than an individual's wealth. For instance, after many years of research it was Alexander Fleming who discovered penicillin, which has helped many generations even after his lifetime. Likewise, Steve Jobs's Apple products outlasted his lifetime for the benefit of the collective ecosystem.

A soulprint can choose to either *consume* all of its wealth in the present moment or *invest* for future use. When you consume a thing, then you use it for yourself and choose not share with others. But when you share it with others (the collective body) then you choose to invest it. For instance, when you keep your money in the bank (collective body) as an investment you chose to share it with others and in turn get returns from it in the future, in terms of interest accruals. The same concept works for your other dots. When you spread happiness then you get back happiness (the same vibrations) from the people when you meet them again at a later stage. When you spread your intelligence in any form, say in the form of a medicine or technology, then you experience a better ecosystem for your self and also leave a better world for the progeny.

The Karmic Cycle

Many investments have already been made '*before you were here*' by your soul and other souls around you. You are thus predestined to receive their *interest payments or benefits* in this lifetime, which is called *destiny*. Your soulful actions (or karma) in your past life is experienced in the form of destiny in this lifetime. Your yesterday's hard work becomes your present day's destiny. When you have faith and insight into this *karmic time lag theory*, you will realize your true purpose and your true potential. Once you realize that your reality is created by your own forgotten past actions, you give more power to your present actions in enriching your future. Thus, you can choose to act based on your wisdom in your everyday actions. *You reap as you sow and what goes around comes around* even at the spiritual level. Therefore, the purpose of your life is to not only increase your spiritual wisdom in your current life, and make all your thoughts and actions more illumined, but also increase your collective wisdom to provide higher living for your future. By seeking to connect the dots of your past with your present, you will be able to understand the reason behind the so-called random events in your life. This realization will help you go a long way in making your life focus towards soulful living. In this way, *theory of karma does not take the power from your hands but rather it gives it back to you to create your own destiny!*

You can never deceive the cosmic science or the spiritual realm as each of your actions will have a commensurate reaction. You may gather ill-gotten wealth in your lifetime and leave it behind for your family to enjoy it, but it is possible that the collective body does not let them be in a happy or peaceful state and perhaps reverberate the negative karma back to them. The Universe captures the intentions of all acts and then you in the way of destiny experience a commensurate reality. After knowing this spiritual fact, would you ever want to leave behind problems and challenges for your loved ones in form of any ill gotten wealth or trappings of your ego?

Protect Your Destiny

Should you bear the brunt of the wrongful deeds of other people around you? Will the misdeeds of your neighbours or your community come back to you as unfavourable events?

Each cell in the human body is a complete unit as well as interconnected with the other cells to form a bigger body. If one cell becomes cancerous then other cells around it also get infected with cancer. The collective body is made up of all the individual soulprints. Your actions affect your fate and also affect the collective fate. Although, other people's actions primarily affect them but they also influence your existence in certain measure. For instance, if a country faces infighting then it calls to reason that such cancerous cells could spread internationally and give rise to terrorism. Thus, other countries too have to pay the social and economic price of wrongful internal affairs of a country and each country should strive to maintain peace in other countries. The collective actions affect every individual and the individual affects the collective in requisite measure. *Hence, an individual should look at enhancing the collective spiritual wealth along with enriching one's personal journey as a long-term sustainable solution to soulful living.*

Similarly when there is goodness in the collective, it surely benefits the individual. Therefore, it is in the individual and collective's self-interest to *invest into* the larger ecosystem by spreading their light of knowledge and wisdom. The world will benefit from your soulful acts, which in turn will accrue for your advancement.

Be a Change Agent

World has won over me,
I had once won over the world.
Did I not?

People have hurt me,
I had once hurt people.
Did I not?

Friends have ignored me,
I had once ignored my friends.
Did I not?

In equal measure things have come back to me,
But I want more than what I have got.
Do I not?

I still feel envy, anger, greed, sloth and lust,
And make the same mistakes that I earlier forgot.
Do I not?

But now I foster happiness and bliss,

And awaken myself to a new destiny.
Will I not!

Your Life's Higher Purpose

You have to walk your path and at the same time illuminate the path for others. This takes your life's purpose to a higher level of existence and answers the existential question of 'why' of your being. Sharing with others is a spiritual investment that you make in the interconnected world. The purpose of the *soulprint is* to make the world a better place. The following story demonstrates this fact.

Monk Kabir was visiting his friend Mukesh in a nearby village. Mukesh's house was the biggest and the most lavish in the village. Mukesh was greatly attached to his village and chose to live there even after getting educated from the finest university abroad. Mukesh served Monk Kabir the best of meals and gave him the finest of linen to rest on at night. After dinner, when Monk Kabir went outside for a stroll he saw people in the neighbourhood scrimmaging over food. The next morning, he told Mukesh that he had a dream the previous night, which revealed that Mukesh would not live long. However, the good news was that his next birth will be in the same village but in a different house. Mukesh was very happy with the prediction and in zest started to look for a suitable house in the village. To his dismay, he could not find any household worthy of his rebirth. He was astounded to discover the rampant poverty in his village. He approached Monk Kabir with his predicament and prayed for a solution.

Monk Kabir advised Mukesh to make his life's purpose bigger. Instead of only increasing his personal wealth, he also needs to work towards making the village more prosperous and illumined. When the whole village becomes a better place then Mukesh's rebirth can happen in any of the houses and should not be a matter of concern. Mukesh realized the importance of a collective spiritual body and started sharing his knowledge, wisdom and wealth for the progress of the whole village. In a few years, the village was transformed into a better place not only for Mukesh's own possible rebirth, but also of other deserving souls. This outlook should not be limited to only one's village, town, city, or country but applies to the world as one huge global village!

Just like you *invest* in the collective environment, you can *overdraw* from it. You have to pay back to the system what you might have overdrawn in the past. This means that, when any past overdue payments accrue in your karmic account, you might experience unfavourable circumstances in your present life and without realizing this truth you get disappointed to have been dealt a losing hand of cards. What can you do in such an uncomforting eventuality?

The journey outside starts from within. If you find your self surrounded by cactus plants then all you can do is to plant (say) mango trees! There is no use of wasting time in complaining about the prickling cactus at this point. What you can do is to make the most of a crisis and look inwards and correct your inner dots instead of blaming your circumstances or the environment or fighting with others. Someone once said, 'Never let a good crisis go to waste', which is a useful tenet for an individual facing hardships.

Inner reformation leads to outer transformation. By choosing to better yourself, you choose to lead an exemplary life and inspire others. The spiritual science of the karmic theory is always at work. This wisdom puts back the power in your hands even during difficult circumstances. Consciously choose to be a change agent by leading a soulful life. For instance, you might have a choice to work either for a tobacco company or a publishing house. If you make the first choice, then you will contribute towards spoiling the collective health and if you choose the latter then you will spread knowledge and wisdom. Your soulfulness has a domino effect on all facets of your life. Interestingly, this phenomenon has been gaining traction in the financial markets context of company valuations and is referred to as sustainability index, in other words, company's level of alignment with its ecosystem. This thought reflects in certain measure in the stock market valuations of companies like Marlboro and Coca-Cola vis-à-vis Tesla and Google.

You Can Keep Your Ferrari (If You Have One)

You do not have to give up your wealth or stop creating it to attain spiritual advancement. The thought of renunciation of the material wealth is completely misplaced as the future generations will benefit from the wealth created by you both at the collective and individual levels. For instance, wealth created by companies like Google or Wikimedia Foundation ensure that every successive generation will have more and better access to information and hence a higher living experience.

When you work or live for purely selfish reasons then you are wasting your life, as neither your soul nor the world becomes a better place. If you do not contribute to your spiritual advancement or generate collective material wealth, then you will surely have a lesser life experience in this life as your inner world would not have progressed any and perhaps even your next life will be devoid of a higher spiritual quotient or consciousness at its start. Negating the material world for spiritual pursuits is the fundamental mistake many soulprints make. Thus, advancing in the collective material realm and in the individual spiritual world, with soulfulness, should be the purpose of one's life.

Rebirth: Believing The Belief

There is reference to two kinds of rebirths, one is the physical rebirth and the other is the spiritual rebirth. Spiritual rebirth is when one awakens and opens one's awareness to the spiritual realm. This spiritual birth marks the beginning of the path of one's spiritual evolution. In Judaism and Christianity, the believers perform an anointment ceremony by rubbing consecrated oil on the forehead of a newborn to mark a healthy spiritual journey.

In certain traditions of Hinduism, spiritual birth is celebrated at a very young age for any awakened soul or devotee or a brahmin, by adornment of a sacred thread in the ceremony called 'Upanayanam', a Sanskrit word meaning 'to start on the journey towards enlightenment'. Here the seeker is made to wear a 'janaeu', a loose strand of white thread, around his shoulder and waist to mark one's enunciation on the spiritual path. The ceremony is symbolic and the ritualistic practice points to one's inner journey.

The physical rebirth refers to the concept that no energy is ever wasted in the cosmos. Everything revolves, and evolves in the Universe. Energy is never lost or gained but simply changes from one form to another. Likewise, to assume that spiritual wisdom is destroyed at the end of one's life would perhaps not be a prudent disposition. In this reference, rebirth pertains to the fact that one's soul does not die on the death of the person and manifests itself again into reality as consciousness of a foetus in the mother's womb. The previous body, life breath, emotive and the intellect dots get destroyed with the earlier lifetime and only the soul or consciousness moves to the new life form, hence we don't remember any of our past events. However, the soul's realizations are taken forward in the next lifetime on its physical rebirths to evolve the soulprint further. All the soft attributes of the body dot like name, family name, relationships and the hard attributes like money, property, shares, gets left behind in the last lifetime. Hence, we should not get attached to the material wealth as it is transitory in terms of the soul and thus, we need to choose to share it with others like the Mukesh's predicament. You need to focus on your awakening along with creation of collective material wealth in creating a higher life experience for your future.

However, many religions like Judaism, Christianity, Islam and Buddhism believe that there is no rebirth and there is only one life. This perspective can also be beneficial as one is forced to put complete focus on one's actions in the present life. After all, this body dot has just one life, and one should enjoy and accomplish most from it. Even Parkinson's Law supports such a philosophy as work expands to fill the time available for it and one's bucket list never gets looked at until the twilight years. The concept of *terminal velocity*, that is, one acts the most when one sees the end in sight, does give the impetus to do what one has to do in the current lifetime. In this way, a soulprint can make most of the current lifetime. This works wonders as one's lifetime gets maximized as well as the quality of one's engagement with inner dots is enhanced. In this belief, there is no complacency as there is no availability of future lifetimes to walk on one's soulful path. Each religion has its own discourse on the theory of spiritual evolution based on its founders. For instance, Gautama Buddha attained enlightenment in one lifetime and thus Buddhists believe in the possibility of attainment of nirvana in one life. To aspire to be like Gautama Buddha is a choice all soulprints or practising Buddhists make for themselves.

However, since there is only one lifetime, the difference between intellect and the soulprint is unascertainable as the salt (ego) stays mixed with the water (soul). This makes one's spiritual pursuit blinded by the limited intellect's vision in place of limitless soulfulness.

One lifetime might be enough to complete one's soulful journey, if one awakens his soulprint and evolves it. However, belief in rebirth along with focus on maximizing current lifetime realizations is the way forward for a complete soulful life.

Ram Rajya and You

The idea of Ram Rajya or collective goodness means a safe, free and truthful environment in the society. Everyone needs to be generous in sharing his or her realizations and spiritual work in attainment of such an utopian place. As per Hinduism, one's spiritual and material wealth should be shared with everyone, and not just your family or friends or community, because a soul can be born anywhere on the planet and into any family or community. So we need to take philanthropic decisions as a win-win proposition for everyone in the world irrespective of our caste, creed, religion, country etc.

For a favourable destiny tomorrow, you have to invest in enriching your soulfulness today. Growth of the individual spiritual world and collective material world is the *real* investment of a soulprint carried on by inculcating the virtues of Karma Yoga, Gyana Yoga, Bhakti Yoga and Dhyana Yoga. Soulprints which are struggling with the basic necessities in reconciling the two worlds choose to consume more whereas more evolved soulprints choose to invest handsomely in both the worlds. *Live today to fight tomorrow* is as important for a soulprint as *sacrifice today for a better tomorrow. Rationality works better with compassion as its goal.* The ecosystem evolves when everyone evolves together, that is, *one for all and all for one!* A balanced approach between investment (soulful) and consumption (living) is the balance we seek in our path to soulful living!

15

LET THE MOON LIGHT YOUR UNIVERSE

Earth's relationship with the moon has been the focus of spirituality over centuries. There have been two external sources of light for the earth, the sun and its reflected light by the moon. The moon by shining in the night sky gives us both light and assurance that the sun's light is still shining for us. Since the earth is a complete living being with a soul, it only calls to reason that the moon will also be a connected to it spiritually. Both of them are completely in sync with each other and the moon fulfils an important spiritual void in earth's existence

Earth-Moon Dynamics

In the spiritual realm, the earth is a complete being and the moon is its nearest relative. It is amazing to see the beautiful, systematic relation the earth and the moon have. The moon is rotating, revolving as well as tilting towards the earth in a synchronized way just like the earth is rotating, revolving and tilting towards the sun. Both have elliptical orbits around their respective centres, that is, the earth's centre is the sun and the moon's centre is the earth. The moon *rotates* on its axis at just the right speed so that when it *revolves* around the earth, we see the moon's only one side called 'its near side'. Interestingly, it takes approximately 27.3 days for the moon to revolve around the earth and it takes exactly the same time for the moon to rotate on its own axis!

The moon and its movements have been part of mankind's spiritual evolution over thousands of years. The moon had been the key timekeeper before the advent of the solar calendar from 1st century. All throughout history, the moon's position has marked major events in human spiritual practices. Lunar cycles still mark the onset of many of the festivals in both Eastern and Western religions (except for Christianity) and their spiritual branches. With the spread of the Roman Empire and the increase in the understanding of the cosmos, the sun took away the importance of the lunar cycles. But we still follow the lunar cycle in our daily spiritual life even today. So what is so special about the lunar cycles?

For one, the moon is the biggest object one sees in the sky albeit at night that changes in a consistent manner. This helped people to keep a track of a set of 28 days at a time and that too at any place on the Plant Earth. Islam's Eid ul fitr and, Judaism's Passover and all festivals of Hinduism are celebrated in sync with the lunar movements because of this reason.

In the lunar system, 'time period' is understood as periods of time where a distinct change has occurred in the season pattern between a full moon and a new moon (moonless night), which is of approximately 29.5 days. As per the Vedic wisdom, every two complete lunar cycles mark a distinct change in the weather pattern to be called a separate season. Thus, the harvesting and reaping times are more closely aligned with the waning and waxing of the moon due to its influence on the water element of the planet. Both philosophically and scientifically, the moon connects to the emotive body on earth, as harvesting periods are monetarily associated with joy and growth throughout the world. The new seasons are started not only by the earth's tilt towards the sun causing the solstice and equinox but also from the moon's effects on earth due to its elliptical orbit and its tidal connect with the earth. The sun regulates the 'fire' (or heat) element whereas the moon modulates the 'water' (or cool) element on earth.

In addition, the moon's gravitational pull causes high and low tides on earth. Isn't it magical to have an element that has magnetic like affect on water that too from such a distance? The moon also influences the blood flow in our bodies as the human body has 70 per cent water content similar to the earth's constitution. Often moonlight, independent of the tides, signals the start of a species-wide reproductive marathon especially for oceanic animals. As the heart beats in a human body and controls the blood flow, comparably the moon (though external) acts as a water pump or a liquid regulator for the earth. Even the menstrual cycle is connected to the lunar time period of fourteen days. Moon has a deeper effect than we realize, on earth and its beings, on both physical and emotive levels.

The moon stabilizes the earth's rotational pull. The earth is tilted along its polar axis, circling the sun at an angle of about 23 degrees. The moon acts as an anchor, preventing the earth from varying its axial tilt by more than a degree or two. Thus, the moon helps to keep the earth from wobbling on its axis under its own force when it rotates and revolves.

The earth primarily has two complete sources of energy—the sun and earth's internal core (magma), which can be called the earth's life force. The moon acts as an additional 'partial' source of energy. This indirect solar energy provides the earth with an extra boost especially on a full moon night. Moreover, sunlight is associated with hot energy whereas moonlight is referred to as the cool energy source. The more incidence of light is on the moon from the sun, the more energy gets reflected back to the earth that is, the fuller the moon gets, and the stronger its effects.

The 'Moons' in Your Life

A seeker can learn from the earth-moon relationship as they are more evolved than us. Just like Planet Earth, we too get our spiritual energy from two sources: one is internal (our life force or soul) and the other is external, that is, our connection to the Super Soul. However, just as the earth has an additional energy source in the form of the moon, you too need to recognize the sources of additional energy in your life. It is a blessing to have additional sources of energy as the Universe is about energy utilization and its use in our evolution.

A Million-Realization Question is: Who all can be the additional sources of energy in your life? As it is important to broaden your perspective and see the earth as a higher living being, likewise you need to broaden your vision to *see people around you* as 'moons' in your spiritual universe. Your family, friends, associates, followers (on twitter!) and even your acquaintances are the 'moons' in your spiritual life. Just like the moons of a planet, they are 'moons' of your soulprint.

Planet Saturn has sixty-two moons and Jupiter has seventy-nine moons of various sizes. Similarly a soulprint can have as many moons as one wishes and this count differs for all beings. Each soulprint chooses the moons for itself. You choose to relate to some moons in your life, and some moons choose you. The 'moons' that you have are the significant people in your life, who come and go based on their own trajectories. Each moon impacts your journey differently, just like the different sizes of the moons of Jupiter. Their impact can be as per the relationship *you choose to nurture* with them and can be understood as the 'soulful distance' of these moons to you. Moreover, every soulprint in your life has different energy levels. They too are connected to the Super Soul in their own way, and the more illumined and illuminated these people are within, the *fuller moon* they become for you, giving you their energy and wisdom. Your choice of the moons and the effort you put in maintaining these relationships lead to your all-round spiritual, intellectual, emotional and physical development. There is a place and a reason for all the moons in your life and when you accept this fact then you can work on your *evolution through interactions with each one of them.*

The Way Forward

You too can be like a moon in the lives of others if you share your wisdom and help them in their advancement. By creating symbiotic relationship with others, including strangers, you can create a spiritual ecosystem similar to the eternal cosmos. When you realize that these moons, orbiting around you, are perhaps like 'full moons' shining their light on you in your darkest hours then you feel grateful and blessed to have them in your universe. To have an enlightened universe of such illuminated and illumined people around you lighting your world is a blessing you can *choose* for yourself. The choice of being happy, thankful and supportive of all the moons in your life is the way forward for an awakened soul.

16

ENLIGHTEN YOUR SOULPRINT

The journey so far has been about discovering and connecting your inner dots and progressed towards seeking the Super Soul and connecting with it. The final phase in the spiritual journey is to attain a higher balanced state of enlightenment where you, the seeker, are completely interactive and aligned with the Universe. In this stage, the soulprint simultaneously seeks growth of the inner bodies as well as of the outer ecosystem. Enlightenment percolates into higher collective spiritual wisdom in the world leading to a higher level of peace and happiness for everyone. This state of existence is encapsulated in the Vedic Mahakavya, 'Aham Brahmasmi!' 'Aham' meaning 'I am' and 'Brahmasmi' meaning 'Bhraman' or 'the cosmos'. Here the two separate beings - 'I' and the 'Universe' are merged into one existence, like a river mixes with the sea and loses its separate identity. The river loses all its characteristics of limited mass, colour, form, but gains the limitless potential of the sea at large.

Enlightened Soul: The Spiritual Warrior

When you reach the state of enlightenment, you lose your self and become one with the cosmos. You can feel that 'I' and the cosmos are one identity in which 'I' does not exist separately. From one perspective your soul is your universe (as its eternal) and your body is its cosmos (as its material existence). Similarly cosmos is the reality of the Super Soul, in shape and form. When the soul departs on death, it becomes part of the Universe and the person's material identity is left behind in the cosmos. However, on attainment of enlightenment, you become one with the Universe in body and spirit while being very much alive!

Becoming one with the Universe does not mean you become God, it means that your *being* is in unison with the bigger existence. It does not mean that the Universe is in unison with you, but rather that you are in complete unison with the Universe. A flower growing in the garden cannot be called the garden itself and a garden without flowers is also incomplete. As the great thinker Rumi said, 'I was lost in God but God is found in me.'

Like a drop of water from the ocean, your soul is a part of the Super Soul. When you are completely embodied then you are completely merged with the Super Soul and you feel limitless existence. Your body dot is limited by time and space. However, in a state of enlightenment due to your spiritual connect with the Universe you feel your potential as 'limitless'. To be limitless is the final destination of evolution of every soulprint.

An enlightened soul spreads the light of wisdom for people around it, like the sun in the material realm. The word 'enlightenment' comes from conjugation of three words, 'en', 'light' and 'enment', which translates as - 'in', 'light' and 'to be' respectively, thus means 'into the light'. It is believed in Hinduism that when an enlightened soul departs, it attains moksha or mukti (release) from the circle of life and death or rebirth. The cycle of rebirth ceases for the enlightened soul, because such souls *do not choose to manifest* back into the material world, as they do not have any more wants and desires to realize.

In other religions, the same concept is understood in their own special ways. For instance, in Christianity, a pure soul once departed is given the title of sainthood to venerate its soulfulness from its contributions to the society. Likewise, in Buddhism, the word 'Bodhisattva' is a conjugation of two words in Pali, 'Bodhi' meaning 'spiritual wisdom' and 'Sattva' meaning 'sat or the truth' meaning 'the knower of the truth' hence an enlightened soulprint. These people are depicted as having a 'halo' around their heads. The halo symbolizes inner awakening, and not necessarily a ring of light as usually depicted in religious paintings.

On the other hand, the ignorance about enlightenment has been misused by fake self-proclaimed spiritual leaders. They preach from their religious egoistic state to spread ignorance and misunderstanding amongst their followers. Due to the ignorance the followers get misdirected to do irrational things to pass the spiritual exam for the heavenly abode in the hope of attaining nirvana, jannat or the seven heavens. However, when you choose to focus on seeking inner awakening and not on external stardom, then you can liberate yourself completely to attain pure bliss.

Stages Towards Enlightenment

A few religions like Jainism have extensively explained the stages towards enlightenment that a person might encounter on his journey. The 'Namokar' mantra in Jainism is one of the oldest and most revered mantras. It is neither a prayer to any God, nor does it ask for any worldly comforts. It simply acknowledges the accomplishments of the soulprint on its evolution and prays for the cosmic blessings for one's inner spiritual journey. Since these stages refer to the seeker's inner development, the mantra focuses on paying obeisance to one's levels of attainment of the inner truth.

This mantra outlines the five stages of spiritual evolution for the seeker, namely, sadhu, upadhaya, acharya, siddha and arihant. You may seek the spiritual wisdom of the mantra for your own spiritual growth and realise its wisdom.

Namo Arihantanam
Namo Siddhanam
Namo Ayariyanam
Namo Uvajjhayanam
Namo Loe Savvasahunam
Eso Panch Namokkaro
Savva Pava Ppanasano
Mangalanancha Savvesim
Padhamam Havei Mangalam

I bow to the arihants, siddhas, acharyas, upadhya and the sadhus.
With this fivefold salutation,
I destroy my ignorance as this mantra is the most auspicious (relevant) one on the spiritual path.

Sadhu

The sadhu's or sadhvi's experience of simplicity and clarity is the first stage for the seeker. In this stage, the seeker experiences soulful living based on morals, values, faith and everyday life of what one deems to be the tenets of general prudence (Jainism in this context). Living a soulful life in itself is not an easy task and requires some discipline and self-control in this first stage on seeker's path.

Upadhaya

The second stage is the experience by the upadhaya, or a person who has the knowledge of the Vedas. When a seeker seeks wisdom from all the sources available to them, like the Vedas, holy texts or even self realizations from meditation then the seeker experiences this second level of inner evolution. Without a higher intellect and spiritual wisdom, you cannot awaken on the inner journey. The first two stages lead to self-realization. The seeker has discovered and connected with their inner dots.

Acharya

The third stage is experienced by the acharya, or a spiritual teacher, who has realized the truth and now chooses to connect with the other souls to spread wisdom. At this stage, the seeker not only shares his wisdom, but also learns from the other souls. This interaction with more people is a critical step towards spiritual development. A spiritual teacher always remains a spiritual student as he seeks to learn from such experiences of teaching to his students.

Siddha

The siddha or the embodied soul experiences the fourth stage. In this stage, the seeker completely connects with the Super Soul. The third and fourth stages lead to a state of embodiment for the seeker.

Arihant

The arihant experiences the fifth stage. An arihant is an enlightened and a completely embodied soul. *Embodiment is a journey whereas enlightenment is the destination for the seeker.* Here the soul and the Universe are in complete unison similar to the state as experienced in the state of samadhi. Once embodied, one has to choose between spending time on one's inner path and a path of spreading spiritual wisdom to others. The journey of investing oneself completely into collective spiritual wisdom is the way taken by the enlightened soul at this stage. A fragrant flower in the world makes it a fragrant place only by sharing what it has; hence, a completely embodied soul makes the world a brighter place by enlightening other souls.

This purpose comes from a deeper realization of a soulprint when it believes and sees the world as one.

Buddha's Ultimate Truth

Once Monk Kabir went to Buddha to get enlightened. He asked Buddha to reveal the ultimate truth about enlightenment, so he too can be enlightened as Buddha. As the monk was relentless in his implorations, Buddha chose to answer him. However, Buddha asked the monk to state the true purpose of seeking enlightenment. Buddha would reveal the ultimate truth only to a 'true seeker', for the ultimate truth cannot be revealed to anyone without a truthful disposition. Monk Kabir confessed that he actually wanted to become a 'bigger' enlightened soul than Buddha. He added, 'I already have many extra realizations of my own that *I* will not share with you, so the ultimate truth will add on to *my* wisdom and will make *me* the most enlightened soulprint.' Monk Kabir thought he could apply the laws of material wealth, which are additive in nature and are self-focused, to attain the state of enlightenment. Buddha realized that the 'I' of Monk Kabir was still not dispelled. The monk had not realized that enlightenment is the state of *being abundant by sharing and not by gathering abundance*. Buddha then shared his wisdom with all his disciples and Monk Kabir as a truly enlightened soul would have done.

Losing oneself to truly find oneself is a million-realization learning. Connecting your limited wisdom of the material world with the 'limitless' wisdom of the Universe is like drinking water from a river. The body can drink only as much water as required at that time. Seekers have desire to seek (drink) all the wisdom out there. As a seeker, you must realize that the river (Universe) belongs to everyone alike and can never be used completely or consumed by any one person. You can only partake from the Universe as much as it is apt for your self and nothing more! Avoid the false ego and share your wisdom. This egoless state of sharing the wisdom was perhaps Buddha's state of mind when he shared wisdom with Monk Kabir.

Enlightenment—A Hard Choice

All seekers, including gurus, pundits or swamis, aspire to be enlightened. However, enlightenment is not as glamorous as it might seem at first. For one, enlightenment of a soul is recognized only after one's death and that too many years after the death. All the enlightened beings such as Buddha, Guru Nanak, Satya Sai Baba came to be truly recognized for their enlightenment by the world many years, even centuries, after they departed.

On the other hand, seeking enlightenment based on the material world's rules of self-consumption and accumulation of wealth does not apply to the spiritual realm, as you have to start by letting go of your body dot. We fret to give up even a part of our body dot (say money) and yet aspire to 'own' the cosmos in its entirety is a contradiction in itself and is not the way of enlightenment. An enlightened soul cannot, and is not, attached to any part of their identity like name, family, community, faith and thus doesn't even associate with their loved ones in any biased way. Thus, completely giving up worldly pleasures for a possibility of future recognition might not be an attractive proposition for anyone seeking enlightenment from a material world perspective.

Thirdly, even an enlightened soul cannot declare himself to be enlightened during his lifetime as that can be misconstrued as their ego. A soul is separated from the body only on death. The enlightened soul in their life journey, remain in-between the material world and the spiritual world and this might not be a coveted position for a soulprint, that is, to be part of neither of the worlds. This is a transformational and transitional phase in spiritual evolution of the enlightened soul and not an easy one to experience.

Lastly, as an enlightened soul focuses on the collective spiritual wisdom they connect with both the lesser evolved as well as higher connected souls. Dealing with this bi-polar levels might not be everyone's cup of tea. For instance, a research scientist might not choose to teach in a kindergarten class.

When you seek these realizations, the respect and gratitude towards people seeking enlightenment also grows in you. Just like the soldiers fighting for their country, the enlightened souls are warriors of the spiritual realm, striving for the greater good.

The Art of Manifesting Your Desires

Acts of such enlightened soulprints, echoes in eternity. The cosmos comes forth with all its might to realize the dreams and initiatives of the embodied souls and more seamlessly for the enlightened ones. The prayers of an enlightened person are in complete sync with the higher wisdom and thus transcend into reality. *This transcendence from the spiritual space to the material world is called manifestation.*

Manifestation is creating reality from your will. It works for everyone alike but more for the embodied and enlightened soul due to their thoughtful and soulful connection and oneness with the Universe. The four tools of soulful living increases your spiritual metabolism, that is, realizing spiritual wisdom, strengthening your faith, maintaining a spiritual practice and surrendering in devotion to the Universe. This helps you to walk on the spiritual path with better direction and power, and works wonders for the science of manifestation to work. The power of both the conscious and the subconscious mind is immense. When you are conscious about your manifestation, you are aware from the perspective of the intellect of what is being created. However, when you subconsciously manifest then you are aware from the perspective of the soul. It is only in the enlightened state can one manifest from both perspectives simultaneously. Magical feats can be achieved in this state such as healing people with a touch or protecting others at times of adversities. In such a state, one can see a complete interconnected ecosystem of the spiritual realm connected with the material world, which connects back to the spiritual realm. For instance, the soulprint is connected to the Super Soul, which manifests prayers into the reality of the material world (the cosmos), which in turn connects to the body sheath of the soulprint as experiences, and that eventually connects back to the soulprint in the form of realizations!

In a state of enlightenment, there is a realization that one is detached and attached at the same time to the world. With the science and power of manifestations, your unlimited ideas get implemented in the material world (limited space) and make you experience a limitless life. Enlightenment spirals life's journey into continuously wishing and experiencing the new universe around the soulprint. The power of spiritual wisdom is equated with a life of abundance. However, the truth about this magical possibility also lies in the realization that the world is already working in perfect balance and harmony, and there is not much one can or should change except choose to spread spiritual wisdom and work towards a more evolved ecosystem.

The Power of Eternal Will

Higher spiritual wisdom manifests into a more sustainable and equitable ecosystem, and thus the world gets created beautifully at a higher level of being for everyone. From nomadic life to the Greek, Roman, Ottoman civilizations, to the British and American world orders, we have seen a marked growth in the collective spiritual wisdom as well as collective material wealth. The material world cannot manifest itself without the eternal *will,* as there can be no creation without the creator. In other words, both spiritual wisdom and material wealth has increased since the nomadic human life.

The ancient seekers knew and believed in the power of manifestation and its truth. They prayed to manifest (perhaps avatars) and set right the world order from time to time. Many spiritual stories refer to correcting the balance between the two worlds by either a king relinquishing his power and wealth or a Super Soul taking birth in form of an avatar or a prophet, thereby taking humans to a higher spiritual wisdom. For instance, Jesus Christ corrected the balance between the power of the Roman Empire and the non-Jewish population of the time. Similarly, Buddha relinquished not only his throne, but also his family in pursuit of enhancing collective spiritual bliss. However, the world has also seen enough misuse and misinterpretation where self-proclaimed 'enlightened souls' become gatekeepers for liberation of other soulprints and have wasted generation of evolution due to falsehood in their intent and practice.

Manifestations happen all the time in your life, but you might not be able to see it. Your present reality is in fact your own manifestation from your past wishes! So the story goes, that once a taxi driver named Kabir was in a marketplace and was looking for a parking space for his car. As he was in a rush, he prayed for an empty slot in desperation. However, as he was about to complete his prayer, a parking space opened up right in front of him. Quickly he apologized and asked God to 'not to bother' as he had found a parking space (on his own!).

Be Careful What You Wish For!

You need to be careful what you seek to manifest. Many a time, you are limited in your intelligence to know what is good for you. Manifestations are immune to being 'good' or 'bad' and simply give the experience to the soulprint to move further in its journey. To assume that a thought so manifested by you is also the eternal's wish and thus a good or a moral thing, might not be correct. In manifestation, you simply ask in the spiritual realm to experience something in the material world. It is like ordering things from Amazon. The marketplace delivers what you order based on your requirements and does not validate that you should or should not consume that product in the first place for your *own good.* Once you get what you ordered you start seeking something else. You might also return the package and not like the experience you got in the first place.

The Real Purpose of Manifestation

All manifestations are reflections of your own inner seeking at a point of time. *Increasing your spiritual wisdom through realizations is the real purpose of manifestation, as no reality will last forever except that of your soul.* Sometimes what you do not want to experience is exactly what the cosmos gives you in order for you to grow out of your fears and inhibitions. Other times, you may desire all the power in the world, but you might not be competent to handle all that extra energy. Hence, manifestation is a science of the spiritual realm, which needs to be used with deference and thoughtfulness.

One human lifespan can be too short to work towards enlightenment if one is not awakened. Time is of no importance in the spiritual realm. If you awaken your soulprint and seek spiritual advancement then anything is possible for your soulprint to realize. However, in today's context, with no personal material benefit whatsoever, and the present societal and educational system neglecting spirituality in general, the expectations from society for people seeking enlightenment as their life goal has dwindled. Maybe like the ancient seekers, we too should pray to the Universe to manifest an 'avatar' or a 'prophet' to guide humans on their journey to embrace enlightenment as a life goal. But till that happens, the power of your journey is in your hands.

When seekers will practise soulful living then the winds of change will start to blow in no time. Without a *soulful living* perspective, you are just floating like a log in the river and bumping into various other logs (dots) floating around you. You must strive to sail through life as one sails through an ocean on a sailboat. You can adjust its direction (your purpose of being here) and your sails (tools of soulful living) depending upon the winds and water currents (cosmic will) in order to take you forward on your path. Higher collective spiritual wisdom will lead to better collective manifestation, thus, making this world a more sustainable, peaceful, happier and a soulful place, that is, the beginning of satyug, or the age of soulful living!

17

CREATE HEAVEN ON EARTH

A journey of a million miles starts with a single step! You have been walking on the path of awakening from many lifetimes. You soulprint has evolved over centuries of life experiences. However, in your present lifetime you might find that your spiritual evolution is deeply influenced by your religious beliefs. Religious beliefs and biases cannot perpetuate limitless existence but you can use them as a starting point for your journey. Once you awaken your soulprint and remove the egoistic religious biases then you can realize the pure spiritual wisdom behind any religion or way of living and truly enrich your life.

> *'There was a time when men followed but one religion. Then they disagreed amongst themselves'*
>
> (Quran 10:19).

The basic difference between the Abrahamic and the Dharmic religions is of the spiritual outlook. The former insists on *believing* in a common book and the latter insist on *seeking* based on common knowledge. This brings to another million-realization question: What is the difference between seekers and believers?

Seekers and Believers

The fundamental difference between the two viewpoints lies in the fact that seekers believe that the spiritual wisdom is evolutionary, whereas, believers believe that spiritual wisdom is a finality (non-evolutionary). Seekers look at the spiritual path from the perspective of the inner selfleading to the Super Soul, whereas believers look at it from the perspective of the Super Soul leading to the inner self. Given the (complete) nature of the Super Soul, believers inculcate fixed thoughts and practices (rituals) on their path to connect with their God. Seekers are more flexible with their points of view and thoughts in order to evolve their spiritual wisdom. Seekers are inquisitive and seek to know more than what is already known, while believers are content with what is already known and believe that they must more diligently practise, what's already been said. Seekers ask questions to ascertain truth for themselves, whereas believers prefer to go 'by the book' and choose to *rest in peace* in their wisdom. Contentment of knowing the final answer and not fretting to seek continuously also has virtues to a certain extent for a soulprint of a believer.

Seekers' wisdom is akin to the evolutionary nature of spirituality or a way of life whereas believers' wisdom is akin to the crystalized nature of spirituality formed into a religion. Seekers' goal and path is ever changing and perhaps more adventurous, whereas believers goal and path are predefined and more stable. Seekers lead their quest and believers follow the quest laid out by someone else.

Both seekers and believers have unequivocal faith and are pure in their inner self, which means their true intentions are placed in the essence of soulfulness. All believers were once seekers and all seekers are susceptible to become believers when they would choose to formalize themselves into a religion. Each soulprint has to decide individually for itself that it chooses to believe, seek or to do both, and to what extent, as no one path is meant for everyone alike. A few soulprints might choose their belief systems to be safe and stable and follow the prescribed path to become believers. Other soulprints can choose to explore (just like new technologies in the material world) and evolve with the times even in their beliefs.

Losing One's Religion

When collectively a community follows the path of believing a set of thoughts (religion) then a gap between their inner realizations and the outer reality is often created. This is because the outer world is ever changing while the inner world has chosen to keep its wisdom static! It takes a landmark event to jolt the society into losing its religious adamancy. This results in creation of a new path for 'higher' and more contemporary realizations towards better living and perhaps a new religion. For instance, with the advent of Internet and video calls, the concept of marrying someone or conducting a religious ceremony over a computer has been left unaddressed by any formalized religion till now. This is a result of what we experience in an evolved material world but the spiritual path followed has been laid out centuries back. Many such evolutionary deficiencies between the two worlds can be seen all around us in our every day living. In past the new path for the ancient believers was led by the revolutionary *seekers* of that time. A Million-Realization Question is who or which kinds of seekers will lead us into the future and how to create a balance between finding contentment in what you believe *and* in seeking new wisdom? This balancing act is a continuous active state of your being and should not be taken for granted. Such inner equanimity and attainment of bliss for self, when done collectively, will result in world peace.

Finding the Spirit of Religions

A million-realization question is whether spiritual wisdom can exist and sustain without a formalized practice, that is, without crystalizing into a religion? Can a religion choose to evolve and upgrade its spiritual technology or does the whole system need to be rebooted altogether to 'install' a higher wisdom? Will the present custodians of religions be open to such an evolutionary and revolutionary idea?

Spiritual Democracy or Religious Imperialism?

In modern times, believers and seekers are not benefiting from the essential goodness of religions across the world. Ironically, this goodness was the reason behind the origin of religions in the first place. The world has evolved and so has the collective intelligence with limited spiritual evolution of its religions. We already see the challenges in the world due to differences amongst religions, which are stuck in their past and perhaps their collective ego. *Past should have a vote in our future and not a veto.*

Interestingly, in the past every time someone tried to bridge the gap between the believers and the (new) seekers, a new religion was born. However, formation of a new religion is not the solution as it might solve the problem temporarily (for a few centuries), but the new founders (themselves) become believers over a period of time and stop questioning their own beliefs. This would create the same challenges as faced in the current times. To stay egoless in your spirituality might be difficult, but is definitely not impossible. We can choose to change our spiritual DNA to quick adaptation based on the principles of Darwin and the survival of quickest to change. Everyday you make choices, so choosing to evolve your spiritual wisdom should not be that difficult in your practice of soulful living. The power to choose one's spiritual freedom leads to *spiritual democracy*, where each person has the right to believe and practice what they choose to believe, without anyone else telling them what is the 'right' path for them. In such a world, one can seek spiritual wisdom from any religion and a religion from any part of spiritual wisdom! The right to choose one's spiritual path comes from learning about the tools of soulful living, which educates and trains the seeker towards basic wisdom of the spiritual realm. In essence, it's your birthright to choose your own spiritual path. Seeking spiritual democracy lets you transcend the material world boundaries, religions and even limitations created by your own yester self.

When you cross-pollinate spiritual wisdom across religions, you get many realizations that can be distilled as pure truth. For instance, all religions value the natural resources, that is, a sustainable environment; respect for elders and also love for children! Finding *commonality of purpose* can be the first step towards evolving your religious thoughts towards spiritual ones. Every seeker can be a reformist as well as a freedom fighter in their discovery of a new personal democratic spiritual order. Practice of spirituality even with one soulprint (yourself) might be the way forward. You can be the great warrior ('Mahavira') on the golden path (Buddha) you so create to walk on for your journey. Following are a few examples of goodness across religions that can be inculcated as a starting point on your soulful journey towards your awakening:

1. Judaism encourages a seeker's outlook. One could picture Jewish worship as an ongoing search for enlightenment. In Judaism it is possible to pray alone, however, it encourages communal worship with a quorum of ten adults. Moreover, a Jew worshipper does not require a rabbi to speak to God even in a formal worship. Also, reading of the holy book on festivals is for 'self study' and seeking purpose only. This thought gives more power to the individual to advance

their spiritual journey and become an agent of change in their communities.

2. In Christianity, the concept of heaven or paradise, exists not in place but in time. For instance, *when* the Judgement Day comes, the believer will attain paradise, which can also be interpreted as an evolutionary concept of the spiritual world and eventually attainment of the highest level.
3. Religious beliefs can evolve. For example, the practice of sati was discontinued with growth in the collective wisdom of the Hindu community. Similarly, Judaism has let go of the need to 'spill blood' in its religious practices.
4. Judaism is an evolving religion with modern thought. For example, many sects of Judaism support gender equality and promote females as rabbis. Some synagogues have even consented to conducting same sex weddings.
5. Islam pioneered the thought of condemning female infanticide in the 6th century. Further, it was the first major religion to grant property rights to women in their husband's estates. It encouraged widows to remarry. The religion also asked believers to take care of orphans as their 'own brothers'. Many religions still do not address such issues.
6. While offering an Islamic prayer, a Muslim sits on the floor many a time with random strangers, and touches shoulders with them thus doing away with the distinction of rich and the poor of the material realm.
7. Protecting the environment has been part of religious practices much before the modern discourse on sustainable environment began. For instance, Hindu married women are encouraged to nurture a banyan tree as part of the Vat Savitri Puja, thus underlining the importance of preserving trees. Avoiding burning of fire crackers on Diwali, or

disposing the idol of Lord Ganesha into soil instead of a water body are a few more relevant examples of mindfulness in today's context. Likewise, in Judaism, a tree plantation ritual is conducted to mark the birth of a baby. For a son, a cedar tree is planted and for a girl a pine or cypress tree is planted.

8. Jainism encouraged prayers instead of conducting animal sacrifices. This act was a radically new thought, and perhaps still is, for a few religions. Jainism further propagates protecting the ecosystem and not to overdraw from its resources or cause any harm to it, in one's self-pursuits.
9. Jainism celebrates the day of Michhami Dukkadam as the day of forgiveness. On this day, the seeker seeks forgiveness from everyone around them, for all acts done knowingly or unknowingly that might have caused them pain. This is a practice of aligning oneself with the Universe to let go of any friction or imbalance cause by one's act earlier. In part, it is similar to the Christian practice of asking 'forgiveness' in the confession box.
10. On festival such as Passover, a Jew can only perform a few prescribed activities, that is, eat, drink, sit and study the holy book. No other activity such as earning money, or cooking, etc. is permitted. Donations to the needy are encouraged at this time in place of excessive self-consumption. This practice not only inculcates introspection, but also stimulates inner spiritual development.
11. Islam encourages the practice of giving alms to the needy according to one's own wealth. Both rich and not-so-rich are expected to donate a certain proportion of their wealth. The thought of contributing irrespective of one's stature to the collective wealth is the way ahead for humanity.
12. The holy places of worship like the synagogues are more

like community centres fulfilling a multitude of communal needs like study, research and social interaction. Moreover, at many such places the clergy are like spiritual coaches who double up as guides of the holy texts for the believers and are not considered mediators between them and God.

13. In Judaism, the local vernacular is acceptable for saying prayers for worship, which brings back the focus on the wisdom of what is being said rather than how it is being said. In a Jewish prayer, *kavanah* (the Hebrew word for intention, or purpose) is given prime importance. In its simplest meaning, it refers to concentrating on the piety of the thought in the performance of a religious act and ensuring that it does not devolve into rote mechanical action.
14. In Sikhism, sewa or selfless service of others is given great prominence as it teaches compassion towards strangers. Acts of cleaning the places of worship, by the believers themselves, as well as cooking and serving at community kitchens to give free food to the needy are wonderful soulful practices.
15. Christianity was the biggest reformist movement of its time. It encouraged excellence in intellect (mathematics, architecture) as well as in emotive field (arts, paintings) along with faith and devotion towards the Super Soul. This was a good way of embracing change and newness by a religion while keeping the spirit of faith alive.
16. Buddhism introduced the concept of dana or donation where a monk would share his spiritual wisdom without any expectation of payment, and at the same time the seeker would benevolently donate as per his means on his own. This was a revolutionary concept of its times and made the spread of knowledge soulful as well as upkeep

of an institution intellectually possible.

The 21st century is very different from the previous ones. With the increase in penetration of technology and international travel, the world has become smaller and flatter. The freedom to make one's life choices is coming back to the individual level, and they can choose what to believe and follow for their soulprint to awaken. Every soulprint has a different journey to experience and new realizations to observe. What is required is the *will* to evolve the inner self. This can be done by a *reformist attitude towards the inner self*. Every individual has a choice to be either an agent of change for themselves and their religion, or to let their beliefs stagnate for their future generations. The change in the collective body starts from an individual. This path has been shown before by spiritual leaders such as Guru Nanak, Gautam Buddha and Adi Shankaracharya.

eDemocracy–A Virtual Heaven

Due to explosion of technology, a virtual world in a new dimension has formed. This virtual world along with the evolution of personal interconnectivity in form of individual smart phones, apps, personal YouTube channels, has empowered individuals to snowball their thoughts into movements for societal change. What is required is piety and *will*, to make this world a better place by believing in the possibility that it can happen. You can use the offline channels like writing and exchanging books, spiritual congregations (satsangs) and also make religious places as spiritual fitness centres for your advancement. You can also create and follow your own *personal religion of one soulprint* in the virtual world. You can seek your inner development and at the same time connect with the other soulprints who might be experiencing similar life choices as your own. Virtual space provides limitless possibilities to overcome barriers across dimensions of time and space, as well as absolve the societal resistances that a few might face on their new path. Small thoughts can domino into bigger goals. In this way, instead of getting burdened by the collective religious imperialism you can focus on your individual spiritual liberation.

Procreate

Spiritual democracy is the creation of a new world order based on the right to *procreate, protect and propel* one's soulprint for progress. With procreation, we try to ensure that our evolution both materially and spiritually is secured for the foreseeable future. This is one of the reasons we must try to save every species from extinction, and to preserve its spiritual wisdom in physical form for our future generations. Like all colours of the rainbow together make up for the complete sunlight and without any one colour, the white light will not be complete. Comparably, each colour (soulprint) has to sustain to complete the ecosystem in the Universe. Procreation and protection of all spiritual DNAs is the fundamental right of every soulprint.

Protect

Protection of each soulprint is essential to sustain all life forms in their natural habitat. This means, one's path cannot limit the others, hence all soulful thoughts and actions should be based on the protection and sustainability of the micro and the macro ecosystem.

Propel

It is important to propel the soulprint, to grow and evolve itself. Blissful existence along with collective evolution of both the worlds is the only purpose of why we are here. As we have progressed over centuries, more than six billion human soulprints have started to live in relative peace and harmony when compared to the earlier times, when few million people existed and faught with each other ad nauseum.

Discover Your Own Special Path

Spiritual democracy at the individualistic level gives the power to the individual to reform one's religious beliefs and become an example for others. After all, the only person who has to benefit from this inner journey is you, so the only person who first needs to reform is yourself! Seek your own truth and do not blindly follow or emulate others' paths because each one of us has their own calling. Even your children cannot walk on your path as they have their own soulprint to live by, and you can only share your life experiences and realizations with them. Moreover, the times will change and today's wisdom might not be relevant tomorrow and every new generation will need to continuously upgrade itself. So, only thing you can do to change the future is to create a culture of egoless seeking of spiritual wisdom for the future generations.

Awakening your soulprint is a journey that starts from realizing spiritual wisdom, strengthening your faith in the Universe, surrendering in complete devotion towards your calling and sincerely pursuing your spiritual practices. These simple tools give impetus to your spiritual metabolism that creates the path of soulful living not only in your everyday life, but also in the lives of all other soulprints, inspiring them to live together in a beautiful limitless world creating a heaven on earth!

ACKNOWLEDGEMENTS

I am grateful to many people who have been part of my soulful journey.

Firstly, I would like to thank the Universe for giving me this lifetime and enriching it with extraordinary experiences. My present day reality has been a wonderful manifestation filled with sparkling realizations. My journey reaffirms my belief that I am unique, just like all other soulprints on the planet, who are treading their own soulful paths.

I am filled with gratitude towards my great great grandfather Shri Lala Rai Bhadur Baij Nath for his writings and teachings to the world. Out of the many books he had written more than a hundred years ago, the one that kindled my spirit the most was his beautiful English translation of the Adhyatma Ramayana, written originally in Sanskrit. His life has not only illumined my soulprint with pure Vedic wisdom, but also taught me the virtues of soulful living.

I would like to thank my father late Shri Yogeshwar Nath (a true Hanuman devotee) and my mother Smt Anjala for inculcating faith and belief in me for the Almighty from a very early age. A man without faith is like a sailboat at sea without the wind or a compass.

I am indebted to Shri Ved Prakash and Smt Mohini for showing me the way of Krishna bhakti and teaching me the essence of true devotion. Prabhu Ved Vyas Das (his Deekshit name), discourses on the Gita and his in-depth study of the Vedas has enlightened my world limitlessly.

I would like to thank my wife, Bhawana for her unshakeable support and for being a confidante to my seeking. I am also thankful to our two wonderful kids, Aviraj and Vasvi, for innocently asking me many questions about the Universe as these gave me the impetus to refine my study into simple answers.

I am grateful to my sister Sangeeta and my brother Ashish for providing a soulful environment at home filled with love and thoughtfulness.

I am obliged for the honest hard work put into this book by Priyanka Swarup and Ruchika Gupta. They tirelessly read and edited my writings and continuously encouraged me on this new journey of writing my first book.

I would like to thank Rupa Publications and its team, Kapish Mehra and Dibakar Ghosh, for believing in me and making this book a reality. I appreciate their sincerity in maintaining the true spirit of the book. Their unrelenting focus in spreading knowledge through books to many soulprints over the years is truly commendable.

Lastly, I want to thank the spiritual leaders who have chosen the higher path to spread their wisdom to seekers like me. These enlightened spiritual warriors have silently given up their lives for the collective spiritual evolution to make this world a better place.

BIBLIOGRAPHY

Ashley-Farrand (Namadeva), Thomas. *Mantra Meditation*. Mumbai: Jaico Publishing House, 2017.

Baij Nath, Rai Bahadur, trans. *Adhyatma Ramayana*. New Delhi: Oriental Books Reprint Corporation, 1979.

Bharat Soka Gakkai. *Basics of Buddhism*. New Delhi: Eternal Ganges Press: 2018.

Bhavnagari, Khorshed. *The Laws of the Spirit World*. Mumbai: Jaico Publishing House, 2018.

Chiplunkar, Suman K. *Mudras and Health Perspectives*. Bengaluru: Vasantha Prakashan, 2018.

Dawood, N.J., trans. *Koran*. United Kingdom: Penguin Books, 1980.

Hirschi, Gertrud. *Mudras: Yoga in Your Hands*. Sri Satguru Publications, Delhi, 2000.

Holy Bible. Secunderabad: The Gideons International, India, 2009.

Jain Philosophy and Practice -1. Raleigh: Jaina Education Committee Federation of Jain Association in North America, 2007.

Long, Jeffery D. *Jainism*. New York: I. B. Tauris & Co. Ltd, first South Asian edition, 2010.

Osho. *The Hidden Harmony: Talks on Heraclitus*. Pune: Osho Media International, 2017.

Pattanaik, Devdutt. *7 Secrets of Vishnu*. Chennai: Westland Ltd, 2011.

———— . *My Gita*. New Delhi: Rupa Publications, 2015.

Radhakrishnan, S. *Principal Upanishads*. Noida: Harper Collins, 2018.

Rai, Roopa. *The Gita for Children*. Gurgaon: Hachette India, 2015.

———. *The Vedas and Upanishads for Children*. Gurugram: Hachette India, 2019.

Robinson, George. *Judaism*.New York: Ataria, 2016.

Sadhguru. *Engineering: A Yogi's Guide to Joy*. Gurugram: Penguin Random House India, 2016.

Snelling, John. *The Buddhist Handbook: A Complete Guide to Buddhist Schools, Teaching, Practice and History*. Rochester, Vermont: Inner Translation, 1998.

Sri Aurobindo. *Integral Healing. Compiled from the Works of Sri Aurobindo and the Mother*. Puducherry: Sri Aurobindo Ashram Publication Department, 2019.

Sri Aurobindo and the Mother. *Growing Within: The Psychology of Inner Development*. Compiled by A.S. Dalal. Puducherry: Sri Aurobindo Ashram Publication Department, 2018.

Swami Prabhupada, A.C. Bhaktivedanta. *Krsna-lila: The Childhood Pastimes of Lord Krishna.* New Delhi: The Bhaktivedanta Book Trust International, Inc., 2008.

———. *Bhagavad Gita: As It Is*. Mumbai: The Bhaktivedanta Book Trust, 1983. Vilas, Shubha. *Bhagavad Gita*. New Delhi: Finger Print Belief (Prakash Books India), 2018).